Wok Cookbook for Beginners

225 Quick and Healthy Recipes to Stir-Fry, Steam and Sauté at Home. Unlock the Secrets of Easy and Delicious Restaurant Dishes

Table of Contents

Introduction

Welcome to the thrilling world of wok cooking! This cookbook is your gateway to a culinary escapade brimming with vibrant flavors, aromatic dishes, and the unique speed and efficiency of this iconic Asian cookware. Tailored for beginners, we've assembled a collection of 225 quick and healthy recipes that capture the essence of restaurant-quality meals, all within the cozy confines of your home.

Envision turning ordinary ingredients into extraordinary dishes with a simple sizzle and stir. With a wok, you can unlock a myriad of possibilities, from classic stir-fries that burst with flavor to delicate steamed creations that preserve nutrients and tantalize taste buds. Whether you're a solo diner seeking quick and satisfying meals or a family looking for wholesome and delicious options, this cookbook has something to offer everyone.

We'll guide you through the essential techniques, from the art of high-heat cooking to the balance of flavors. You'll learn how to select the perfect wok for your needs, properly season it for optimal performance, and confidently handle this versatile tool. No more intimidation, just pure cooking joy!

Inside these pages, you'll discover a diverse range of recipes inspired by cuisines from across Asia. From the fiery heat of Sichuan to the subtle elegance of Japanese flavors, we've curated a menu that caters to every palate. You'll find it all here whether you crave spicy stir-fries, aromatic curries, or light and refreshing noodle dishes.

So, gather your ingredients, fire up your wok, and embark on this culinary journey together. With this cookbook as your companion, you'll soon create restaurant-worthy dishes that impress your friends and family. Get ready to experience the magic of wok cooking!

Chapter 1: Wok Essentials

The History of the Wok

The wok, a seemingly simple, bowl-shaped cooking vessel, is a culinary powerhouse. It is the cornerstone of many Asian cuisines, from the fiery stir-fries of China to the aromatic curries of Thailand and the vibrant noodle dishes of Japan. Its versatility, coupled with the high-heat cooking it facilitates, has given rise to a diverse and dynamic culinary tradition that continues to evolve while honoring its rich history.

Geographical and Cultural Setting

The wok's origins are believed to lie in China, where it was used as early as the Han Dynasty (206 BC – 220 AD). Its design, with a rounded bottom and sloping sides, was perfectly suited to the intense heat of traditional Chinese stoves fueled by wood or charcoal. The wok quickly became an indispensable tool in Chinese kitchens, and its use spread throughout Asia, adapting to the unique ingredients and culinary traditions of each region.

Historical Influences

Indigenous Ingredients: Asian cuisine, as a whole, is rooted in the abundant and diverse ingredients found across the continent. Rice, noodles, fresh vegetables, seafood, and various proteins like pork, chicken, and tofu have been staples for centuries. The wok's ability to quickly cook these ingredients over high heat ensured they retained their nutritional value and flavor while minimizing the need for excessive oils or fats.

Cultural Exchange: The Silk Road, a network of trade routes connecting the East and West, played a significant role in shaping Asian cuisine. Spices like cumin, coriander, and chili peppers were introduced from India and the Middle East, adding new dimensions of flavor to traditional dishes. Similarly, the arrival of Europeans in the 16th century brought ingredients like potatoes, tomatoes, and corn, which were gradually incorporated into local cuisines.

Evolution of Cuisine

Historical Events: Throughout history, events like wars, famines, and economic shifts have all left their mark on Asian cuisine. During times of scarcity, resourceful cooks found ways to stretch ingredients and create dishes that were both nutritious and flavorful. In times of prosperity, new ingredients and techniques became available, leading to further culinary innovation.

Modernization: In recent decades, Asian cuisine has undergone a significant transformation, with the rise of fusion cuisine and the global popularity of dishes like sushi, ramen, and Pad Thai. Despite these modern influences, the wok remains at the heart of many Asian kitchens, both as a symbol of culinary tradition and a tool for modern culinary innovation.

Key Figures and Movements

While it's difficult to pinpoint specific individuals who have single-handedly shaped wok-based cuisine, numerous chefs and food writers have played a role in preserving and promoting traditional techniques while also introducing new and exciting variations. In recent years, there has been a growing interest in sustainable and healthy eating, which has led to a renewed focus on fresh, locally sourced ingredients and traditional cooking methods like wok cooking.

The recipes in this cookbook are a testament to the dynamic and ever-evolving nature of wok-based cuisine. They showcase the versatility of the wok, its ability to enhance flavors, and its potential to create delicious and healthy meals. By exploring these recipes, you are not just cooking a meal; you are participating in a culinary tradition that has been shaped by centuries of history, culture, and innovation.

As you embark on this culinary journey, remember that the wok is more than just a pan. It is a symbol of ingenuity, resilience, and the power of food to connect us to our past while embracing the future.

How to Choose the Right Wok for You

The wok, a cornerstone of Asian cuisine, is celebrated for its versatility and efficiency in the kitchen. This simple yet ingenious cooking vessel has a rich history and continues to be a favorite among chefs and home cooks alike. In this article, we delve into the workings of the wok, exploring its design, functionality, and the techniques that make it a culinary essential.

The wok's primary function is stir-frying, a high-heat cooking technique that involves quickly tossing and turning ingredients to cook them evenly and preserve their texture and flavor. However, the wok's versatility extends far beyond stir-frying. It can also be used for steaming, pan-frying, deep-frying, braising, boiling, and even smoking.

Technical Aspects of Wok Cooking

1. **Main Components:**
- **Bowl-shaped Body:** The wok's signature bowl shape allows for efficient heat distribution, ensuring that the entire cooking surface is heated evenly. This is especially important for stir-frying, where high heat is essential for quick cooking and caramelization.
- **Sloped Sides:** The sloped sides of the wok make it easy to toss and stir food, allowing for even cooking and preventing ingredients from sticking to the bottom.
- **Long Handle:** The wok's long handle provides a safe distance from the heat source and makes it easy to maneuver the wok during cooking.

2. **Material Matters:**
- **Carbon Steel:** The traditional choice, carbon steel woks are lightweight, heat up quickly, and develop a natural non-stick patina over time with proper seasoning. They are ideal for high-heat cooking like stir-frying.
- **Cast Iron:** Cast iron woks are heavy and retain heat well, making them great for slow cooking and braising. However, they are heavier to maneuver and require more maintenance.
- **Stainless Steel:** Durable and easy to clean, stainless steel woks are an excellent choice for beginners. They don't require seasoning, but they may not develop the same non-stick properties as carbon steel.
- **Non-Stick:** Non-stick woks are convenient for low-fat cooking, but they are not ideal for high-heat stir-frying as the coating can be damaged.

3. **Size and Shape:**
- **Size:** Wok sizes typically range from 12 to 14 inches in diameter. Consider your household size and stovetop when choosing the size. A 14-inch wok is ideal for family-sized meals, while a 12-inch wok is better for smaller households or those with limited storage space.
- **Shape:**
  - ○ **Round Bottom:** Traditional woks have a round bottom, which is perfect for gas stoves with a wok ring. They offer superior heat distribution but can be unstable on flat-top stoves.
  - ○ **Flat Bottom:** Flat-bottomed woks are designed for modern kitchens and work well on electric and induction stoves. They may not have the same heat distribution as round-bottomed woks, but they are easier to use for beginners.

4. Handle Design:

- **One Long Handle:** This design is traditional and provides good leverage for tossing and flipping ingredients. It can be a bit unwieldy for storing, though.
- **Two Loop Handles:** These are easier to handle and store, but they don't offer the same leverage for tossing.

5. Additional Considerations:

- **Weight:** Consider the weight of the wok, especially if you plan to do a lot of tossing and flipping. Carbon steel is the lightest, while cast iron is the heaviest.
- **Price:** Woks can range in price from very affordable to quite expensive. Consider your budget and how often you plan to use the wok.
- **Lid:** A lid can be useful for steaming and braising. Some woks come with a lid, while others require you to purchase one separately.

How the Wok Works:

The wok's efficiency lies in its ability to rapidly conduct heat. The round bottom concentrates the heat at the center, while the sloped sides allow for different temperature zones. This means you can cook multiple ingredients simultaneously, searing meats at the bottom and gently cooking vegetables on the sides. The wok's large surface area also makes it ideal for tossing and stirring food, ensuring even cooking and preventing burning.

Tips for Choosing the Right Wok:

- **Cooking Style:** If you plan to do a lot of stir-frying, a carbon steel wok with a round bottom is ideal. For more versatile cooking, a flat-bottomed wok made of stainless steel or non-stick may be a better choice.
- **Experience:** If you're a beginner, a flat-bottomed wok made of stainless steel or non-stick may be easier to handle and requires less maintenance.
- **Care & Maintenance:** Carbon steel woks require seasoning, which is a process of coating the wok with oil to create a non-stick surface and prevent rust. If you're not willing to put in the time for seasoning, choose a stainless steel or non-stick wok.

By considering these factors and choosing the right wok for your needs, you'll be well on your way to mastering the art of wok cooking and creating delicious, healthy meals at home.

How to maintain your Wok

Troubleshooting and maintenance tips are as follows:

- **Seasoning:** If you have a carbon steel wok, it's important to season it properly to prevent rusting and sticking. This involves heating the wok and coating it with oil several times.
- **Sticking:** If food starts to stick, add a little more oil to the wok.
- **Cleaning:** Clean the wok after each use with hot water and a soft sponge. Avoid using soap, as it can remove the seasoning.

By understanding the workings of the wok and mastering the different cooking techniques it allows, you can create a wide variety of delicious and healthy dishes. So fire up your wok and start exploring the exciting world of wok cooking!

Tips for beginners: avoiding common Wok cooking mistakes

Wok cooking is a thrilling culinary adventure, full of sizzling flavors and vibrant colors. But for beginners, it can also be a bit daunting. Fear not! With a few simple tips, you can easily avoid common mistakes and master the art of wok cooking in no time.

1. Not Getting Your Wok Hot Enough

- **The Mistake:** One of the biggest mistakes beginners make is not heating their wok enough. This can result in food that is steamed or boiled instead of stir-fried, leading to mushy textures and lackluster flavors.
- **The Fix:** Crank up the heat! Woks are designed for high-heat cooking, so don't be afraid to crank up your stove too high. The wok should be hot enough that a drop of water sizzles and evaporates instantly when it hits the surface.

2. Overcrowding the Wok

- **The Mistake:** Another common mistake is overcrowding the wok with too many ingredients. This lowers the temperature of the wok and prevents the food from searing properly, resulting in a soggy mess.
- **The Fix:** Cook in batches! If you're cooking a large quantity of food, cook it in smaller batches. This will ensure that everything cooks evenly and quickly, with a nice sear.

3. Not Prepping Ingredients in Advance

- **The Mistake:** Wok cooking is all about speed, so it's important to have all your ingredients prepped and ready to go before you start cooking. This means chopping your vegetables, slicing your meat, and measuring out your sauces.
- **The Fix:** Mise en place! This French term means "everything in its place." Take a few minutes to prep all your ingredients before you start cooking. This will help you stay organized and ensure that your stir-fry comes together quickly and smoothly.

4. Using the Wrong Oil

- **The Mistake:** Using an oil with a low smoke point, like olive oil, can lead to a burnt taste and unhealthy fumes.
- **The Fix:** Choose a high smoke point oil! Oils like peanut oil, canola oil, or grapeseed oil are ideal for wok cooking, as they can withstand the high heat without burning.

5. Overcooking Your Vegetables

- **The Mistake:** Overcooked vegetables become mushy and lose their vibrant color and flavor.
- **The Fix:** Add vegetables in stages! Start with the vegetables that take longer to cook, like carrots and broccoli, and add the quicker-cooking vegetables, like snow peas and bean sprouts, towards the end. This will ensure that all your vegetables are perfectly cooked.

6. Forgetting to Season Your Wok

- **The Mistake:** If you have a carbon steel wok, it's important to season it properly to create a non-stick surface and prevent rust.
- **The Fix:** Season your wok! This involves coating the wok with oil and heating it repeatedly. This process creates a polymerized layer on the surface that prevents food from sticking.

Bonus Tip: Don't be afraid to experiment! Wok cooking is all about exploring flavors and textures. So get creative with your ingredients and have fun!

Chapter 2: Mastering Wok Techniques

Stir-frying

The wok's signature move, stir-frying, is all about high heat and rapid movement.

- **Key to Success:** A screaming hot wok ensures ingredients are seared quickly, locking in flavor and creating that signature *wok hei* (smoky aroma). Constant tossing and stirring keeps food moving, preventing burning and ensuring even cooking.
- **Perfect For:** Tender proteins like chicken, beef, shrimp, and vegetables that cook quickly. Think classic dishes like Kung Pao Chicken, Beef & Broccoli, or Shrimp with Snow Peas.
- **Pro Tip:** Prep all your ingredients before you start cooking. Stir-frying is fast-paced, so having everything ready to go ensures success.

Deep-frying

The wok's depth and wide opening make it an excellent vessel for deep-frying.

- **Key to Success:** Use a deep-fry thermometer to monitor oil temperature and ensure consistent results. Don't overcrowd the wok. Fry in batches for crispy exteriors.
- **Perfect For:** Crispy appetizers like spring rolls, wontons, or even desserts like fried ice cream.
- **Pro Tip:** Use a spider or slotted spoon to carefully lower and remove food from the hot oil.

Steaming

A bamboo steamer basket placed over a wok of simmering water is an easy and healthy way to cook.

- **Key to Success:** Make sure the water level doesn't touch the bottom of the steamer. Keep the lid on to trap the steam and ensure even cooking.
- **Perfect For:** Delicate dishes like fish, dumplings, and vegetables. Try steamed buns, whole fish with ginger and scallions, or vegetable dumplings.
- **Pro Tip:** Line the steamer basket with parchment paper or cabbage leaves to prevent sticking.

Pan-Frying

The wok doubles as a skillet for pan-frying.

- **Key to Success:** Use medium heat and a little oil to prevent food from sticking. Turn ingredients occasionally for even browning.
- **Perfect For:** Crispy exteriors on fish fillets, pancakes, or even larger items like whole fish or omelets.
- **Pro Tip:** Use a wok spatula with a flat edge to easily turn and flip food during pan-frying.

Braising

The wok's ability to hold heat makes it a surprisingly good braising vessel.

- **Key to Success:** Sear meat or tofu first, then add liquid and simmer until tender. Use a lid to trap moisture and ensure even cooking.
- **Perfect For:** Tougher cuts of meat like beef shank or pork belly, as well as tofu. Try red-braised pork belly or soy sauce chicken.
- **Pro Tip:** If your wok doesn't have a lid, transfer ingredients to a pot with a lid for the braising stage.

Smoking

Believe it or not, you can even smoke food in a wok!

- **Key to Success:** Line the bottom of the wok with foil and add wood chips. Place a rack over the chips, add the food, and cover with a lid. Heat the wok and let the smoke do its magic.
- **Perfect For:** Adding a smoky flavor to meats, fish, or vegetables.
- **Pro Tip:** Experiment with different types of wood chips for unique flavor profiles.

Chapter 3: Simple Meals for Beginners

30-minute Dishes for Beginners

Speedy Shrimp Lo Mein

Yields: 2 servings **Prep time:** 10 minutes **Total time:** 25 minutes **Equipment:** Wok, spatula.

Ingredients: 6oz lo mein noodles, 1 tbsp oil, 1/2lb shrimp, 2 minced garlic cloves, 1/2 cup chopped broccoli, carrots, 1/4 cup sliced red bell pepper, snow peas, 3 sliced green onions, 2 tbsp soy sauce, 1 tbsp oyster sauce, 1 tsp sesame oil, 1/2 tsp sugar, 1/4 tsp red pepper flakes.

Instructions: 1. Cook noodles. 2. Whisk 2 tbsp soy sauce, 1 tbsp oyster sauce, 1 tsp sesame oil, 1/2 tsp sugar, and red pepper flakes in a bowl. 3. Heat 1 tbsp oil in a wok over high heat. 4. Stir-fry shrimp for 2-3 min. 5. Remove shrimp. 6. Stir-fry garlic, broccoli, carrots, bell pepper, snow peas 3-4 min. 7. Add noodles, shrimp, white onion parts, and sauce to the wok. 8. Toss. 9. Cook for 1-2 min. 10. Garnish with green onions.

Nutritional info: Calories: 450, Protein: 25g, Carbs: 50g, Fat: 15g, Fiber: 5g.

Weeknight Chicken & Broccoli Stir-fry

Yields: 4 servings **Prep time:** 15 minutes **Total time:** 30 minutes **Equipment:** Wok, spatula.

Ingredients: 1 lb boneless chicken, 1 tbsp soy sauce, 1 tbsp cornstarch, 1/2 tsp sesame oil, pinch of black pepper, 1 tbsp oil, 3 minced garlic cloves, 1 tbsp grated ginger, 1 head broccoli, 1/4 cup chicken broth, soy sauce, 2 tbsp oyster sauce, 1 tbsp honey, 1 tsp cornstarch, 2 tbsp water, sesame seeds, green onions (optional).

Instructions: 1. Combine chicken, 1 tbsp soy sauce, 1 tbsp cornstarch, sesame oil, pepper. 2. Heat the wok. 3. Add oil and chicken. 4. Cook for 5-7 min. 5. Remove. 6. Add garlic and ginger. 7. Cook for 30 sec. 8. Add broccoli and cook 2-3 min. 9. Whisk broth, 1/4 cup soy sauce, oyster sauce, honey, 1 tsp cornstarch, water. 10. Return chicken. 11. Add sauce. 12. Cook for 1-2 min. 13. Garnish. 14. Serve.

Nutritional info: 350 cal, 30g protein, 20g carbs, 15g fat, 4g fiber.

Quick Cashew Tofu

Yields: 2 servings **Prep time:** 10 minutes **Total time:** 25 minutes **Equipment:** Wok, spatula.

Ingredients: 1 block (14oz) tofu, cubed, 1 tbsp cornstarch, 2 tbsp oil, 1/2 cup chopped onion, 2 minced garlic cloves, 1/2 cup chopped red bell pepper, broccoli florets, 1/4 cup cashews, 2 sliced green onions, 2 tbsp soy sauce, 1 tbsp hoisin sauce, 1 tsp rice vinegar, 1/2 tsp sesame oil, red pepper flakes.

Instructions: 1. Toss tofu with cornstarch. 2. Heat oil in a wok. 3. Stir-fry tofu 5-7 min. 4. Remove. 5. Stir-fry onion, garlic, bell pepper 2-3 min. 6. Add broccoli, cook 2 min. 7. Whisk sauces, vinegar, oil, flakes. 8. Return tofu. 9. Add sauce. 10. Cook for 1-2 min. 11. Add cashews and onions. 12. Serve.

Nutritional info: 400 cal, 20g protein, 30g carbs, 20g fat, 5g fiber.

30-Minute Beef and Snow Peas

Yields: 4 servings **Prep time:** 10 minutes **Total time:** 30 minutes **Equipment:** Wok, spatula.

Ingredients: 1 lb flank/sirloin steak, 2 tbsp soy sauce, 1 tbsp cornstarch, 1 tsp sesame oil, 1/2 tsp ginger, pepper, 2 tbsp oil, 3 minced garlic cloves, 1/2 sliced onion, 8oz snow peas, 1/2 sliced red bell pepper, 1/4 cup water/broth, 1 tbsp oyster sauce, 1 tsp sugar, salt, pepper.

Instructions: 1. Marinate beef in 2 tbsp soy sauce, cornstarch, sesame oil, ginger, and pepper for at least 10 min. 2. Heat wok. 3. Add 1 tbsp oil, beef. 4. Cook 2-3 min. 5. Remove. 6. Add remaining oil, garlic, onion. 7. Cook for 1 min. 8. Add peas and pepper, and cook for 2-3 min. 9. Return beef. 10. Add water/broth, oyster sauce, sugar. 11. Season with salt and pepper to taste. 12. Serve.

Nutritional info: 380 cal, 25g protein, 20g carbs, 20g fat, 4g fiber.

Fast & Flavorful Vegetable Fried Rice

Yields: 4 servings **Prep time:** 10 minutes **Total time:** 25 minutes **Equipment:** Wok, spatula.

Ingredients: 3 cups cooked rice, 2 tbsp oil, 2 minced garlic cloves, 1 tbsp ginger, 1/2 cup chopped onion, 1 cup mixed veggies, 2 eggs, 3 sliced green onions, soy sauce, sesame oil (optional).

Instructions: 1. Chop fresh/thaw frozen veggies. 2. Heat 2 tbsp oil in a wok over high heat. 3. Stir-fry garlic, ginger, and white onions for 1-2 min or until fragrant. 4. Push aside, scramble eggs. 5. Add veggies and cook for 2-3 min. 6. Add rice and cook for 3-4 min or until heated through and coated with the oil and flavors. 7. Season with soy sauce. 8. Drizzle sesame oil and add green onions. 9. Serve.

Nutritional info: 300 cal, 8g protein, 45g carbs, 10g fat, 2g fiber.

Easy Teriyaki Salmon

Yields: 2 servings **Prep time:** 10 minutes **Total time:** 25 minutes **Equipment:** Wok, spatula.

Ingredients: 2 salmon fillets, 1 tbsp oil, 1/4 cup soy sauce, 2 tbsp mirin, 2 tbsp sake, 1 tbsp honey/sugar, 1 minced garlic clove, 1 tsp ginger, broccoli florets, snow peas, carrots, bell peppers, sesame seeds, green onions.

Instructions: 1. Pat salmon dry with paper towels to remove excess moisture. 2. Chop veggies. 3. Combine the soy sauce, mirin, sake, honey or sugar, minced garlic, and grated ginger in a small saucepan. 4. Simmer over medium heat and cook for 2-3 min or until the sauce has thickened slightly. 5. Heat oil in a wok. 6. Stir-fry veggies for 3-4 min or until crisp-tender and remove. 7. Cook salmon for 3-4 min/side. 8. Add sauce, cook 1 min. 9. Return the stir-fried veggies to the wok and toss to coat with the teriyaki sauce. 10. Serve over rice/noodles, garnish.

Nutritional info: 400 cal, 30g protein, 20g carbs, 20g fat, 2g fiber.

Simple Sesame Noodles

Yields: 2 servings **Prep time:** 5 minutes **Total time:** 15 minutes **Equipment:** Wok, spatula.

Ingredients: 8oz noodles, 1 tbsp oil, 2 minced garlic cloves, 1 tbsp ginger, 1/4 cup soy sauce, 2 tbsp rice vinegar, sesame oil, 1 tbsp honey/maple syrup, 1/4 tsp red pepper flakes, green onions, sesame seeds.

Instructions: 1. Cook noodles. 2. Heat 1 tbsp oil in a wok. 3. Add the minced garlic and grated ginger to the hot wok. 4. Stir-fry for 1-2 min or until fragrant. 5. Add soy sauce, vinegar, sesame oil, honey/syrup, and flakes. 6. Add noodles and toss. 7. Cook for 1-2 min. 8. Garnish with onions and seeds.

Nutritional info: 400 cal, 10g protein, 60g carbs, 15g fat, 2g fiber.

Kung Pao Chicken in a Flash

Yields: 4 servings **Prep time:** 15 minutes **Total time:** 30 minutes **Equipment:** Wok, spatula.

Ingredients: 1 lb boneless chicken, 1 tbsp soy sauce, 1 tbsp rice wine, 1 tsp cornstarch, white pepper, 2 tbsp oil, 1 tbsp Sichuan peppercorns, 8-10 dried chilies, 3 minced garlic cloves, 1-inch ginger, 1/2 red & green bell pepper, 1/2 cup peanuts, 3 sliced green onions, 2 tbsp soy sauce, 1 tbsp vinegar, 1 tbsp rice wine, 1 tbsp sugar, 1 tsp cornstarch, 1/4 cup water.

Instructions: 1. Marinate chicken in soy sauce, rice wine, cornstarch, and pepper for at least 15 min. 2. Heat a dry skillet over medium heat. 3. Add the Sichuan peppercorns and toast for 1-2 min or until fragrant and slightly browned. 4. Let cool; grind in a spice grinder or mortar, and pestle. 5. Mix sauce ingredients: whisk together the 2 tbsp soy sauce, vinegar, rice wine, sugar, cornstarch, and water. 6. Stir-fry chicken in 1 tbsp hot oil for 3-4 min. 7. Remove. 8. Stir-fry chilies, garlic, ginger for 30 sec. 9. Add peppers and stir-fry for 2-3 min. 10. Return chicken, add sauce and peppercorns, and cook for 1 min. 11. Stir in peanuts and onions for an extra 30 sec. 12. Serve.

Nutritional info: 450 cal, 30g protein, 35g carbs, 20g fat, 4g fiber.

Speedy Sweet & Sour Pork

Yields: 4 servings **Prep time:** 10 minutes **Total time:** 25 minutes **Equipment:** Wok, spatula.

Ingredients: 1 lb pork, 1/4 cup cornstarch, 1 tbsp soy sauce, pepper, 2 tbsp oil, 1 minced garlic clove, 1/2 diced onion, 1 red & green bell pepper, 1 can pineapple chunks, 1/2 cup pineapple juice, 1/4 cup rice vinegar, 2 tbsp ketchup & soy sauce, 1 tbsp sugar, 1 tsp cornstarch, 1/4 tsp red pepper flakes.

Instructions: 1. Coat pork in cornstarch, soy sauce, and pepper. 2. Stir-fry in 1 tbsp hot oil until browned. 3. Remove. 4. Stir-fry garlic, onion, and peppers for 2-3 min. 5. Add pineapple juice, vinegar, ketchup, soy sauce, sugar, and flakes. 6. Thicken the sauce: whisk together the 1 tsp cornstarch with 2 tbsp water. 7. Add the cornstarch slurry to the sauce and cook for 1 min or until the sauce has thickened. 8. Return pork and pineapple. 9. Cook for 1 min. 10. Serve.

Nutritional info: 400 cal, 25g protein, 40g carbs, 15g fat, 2g fiber.

Lemon Garlic Shrimp Scampi

Yields: 2 servings **Prep time:** 5 minutes **Total time:** 15 minutes **Equipment:** Wok, spatula.

Ingredients: 1 lb shrimp, 2 tbsp oil, 4 minced garlic cloves, 1/4 cup white wine, 2 tbsp butter, 1 tbsp lemon juice, 1 tbsp parsley, 1/4 tsp red pepper flakes, salt, pepper, lemon wedges.

Instructions: 1. Pat shrimp dry, season with salt and pepper. 2. Heat 2 tbsp oil in a wok. 3. Stir-fry shrimp until pink. 4. Remove. 5. Add the minced garlic to the wok and cook for 30 sec or until fragrant. 6. Add wine and simmer for 1 min or until the alcohol has evaporated. 7. Add butter, lemon juice. 8. Return shrimp. 9. Add parsley and flakes. 10. Serve with lemon wedges.

Nutritional info: 350 cal, 30g protein, 10g carbs, 20g fat, 1g fiber.

One-Pan Ginger Chicken with Bok Choy

Yields: 4 servings **Prep time:** 10 minutes **Total time:** 25 minutes **Equipment:** Wok, spatula.

Ingredients: 1 lb boneless chicken, 1 tbsp soy sauce, cornstarch, sesame oil, 1/2 tsp ginger, 2 tbsp oil, 2 minced garlic cloves, 1 tbsp ginger, 2 heads baby bok choy, 1/4 cup broth/water, 2 tbsp soy sauce, 1 tbsp oyster sauce, 1 tsp sugar, salt, pepper, sesame seeds, green onions.

Instructions: 1. Marinate chicken in soy sauce, cornstarch, sesame oil, and ginger for at least 10 min. 2. Stir-fry in 1 tbsp hot oil until browned. 3. Remove. 4. Add remaining oil, garlic, ginger. 5. Stir-fry for 30 sec or until fragrant. 6. Add the quartered baby bok choy to the wok and stir-fry for 2-3 min or until slightly wilted. 7. Add broth, soy sauce, oyster sauce, sugar. 8. Pour the chicken broth, soy sauce, oyster sauce, and sugar over the bok choy. 9. Bring to a simmer and cook for 1-2 min or until the sauce has thickened. 10. Season with salt and pepper to taste. 11. Garnish with sesame seeds and sliced green onions. 12. Serve.

Nutritional info: 350 cal, 25g protein, 15g carbs, 20g fat, 4g fiber.

Five Ingredient Wok Recipes

Garlic Ginger Bok Choy

Yields: 4 servings **Prep time:** 5 minutes **Total time:** 15 minutes **Equipment:** Wok, spatula.

Ingredients: 2 lbs bok choy, 1 tbsp oil, 3 minced garlic cloves, 1 tbsp ginger, 2 tbsp soy sauce, 1 tbsp oyster sauce, 1 tsp sesame oil, red pepper flakes, sesame seeds.

Instructions: 1. Separate the bok choy into white and green parts. 2. Cut the white parts into 1-inch pieces. 3. Heat 1 tbsp oil in a wok over high heat. 4. Add the minced garlic and grated ginger and stir-fry for 30 sec or until fragrant. 5. Add white parts and cook for 2 min. 6. Add green parts and cook for 2 min. 7. Add sauces, oil, and flakes. 8. Toss. 9. Garnish with seeds. 10. Serve.

Nutritional info: 100 cal, 4g protein, 7g carbs, 7g fat, 2g fiber.

Spicy Peanut Noodles

Yields: 2 servings **Prep time:** 5 minutes **Total time:** 15 minutes **Equipment:** Wok, spatula.

Ingredients: 8oz rice noodles, 1 tbsp oil, 3 minced garlic, 1 tbsp ginger, 1/4 cup peanut butter, soy sauce, 2 tbsp rice vinegar, 1 tbsp honey/syrup, 1-2 tsp sriracha, 1/4 cup chopped cilantro & peanuts, lime wedges.

Instructions: 1. Cook noodles. 2. Stir-fry garlic and ginger in hot oil for 30 sec. 3. Add peanut butter, soy sauce, vinegar, sweetener, and sriracha. 4. Stir until smooth. 5. Adjust the amount of sriracha to your desired level of spiciness. 6. Add noodles and toss to coat. 7. Cook for 1-2 min. 8. Top with cilantro, peanuts. 9. Serve with lime.

Nutritional info: 550 cal, 15g protein, 70g carbs, 25g fat, 4g fiber.

Honey Soy Salmon

Yields: 2 servings **Prep time:** 10 minutes **Total time:** 25 minutes **Equipment:** Wok, spatula.

Ingredients: 2 salmon fillets, 1 tbsp oil, 1/2 tsp ginger, 2 minced garlic, 1/4 cup soy sauce, 2 tbsp honey, 1 tbsp vinegar, 1 tsp sesame oil, flakes, sesame seeds, green onions, 1/2 cup broccoli, carrots, 1/4 cup snow peas.

Instructions: 1. Pat salmon dry and season with salt and pepper. 2. Heat 1 tbsp oil in a wok over high heat. 3. Cook salmon for 3-4 min/side. 4. Remove. 5. Add the minced garlic and grated ginger to the hot wok. 6. Stir-fry for 30 sec or until fragrant. 7. Add the broccoli florets, chopped carrots, and snow peas to the wok. 8. Stir-fry for 3-4 min or until crisp-tender. 9. Pour the soy sauce, honey, rice vinegar, sesame oil, and red pepper flakes (if using) over the veggies. 10. Stir to combine. 11. Bring the sauce to a simmer and cook for 1-2 min or until slightly thickened. 12. Return salmon and veggies. 13. Cook for 1 min. 14. Garnish with sesame seeds and sliced green onions. 15. Serve.

Nutritional info: 400 cal, 30g protein, 20g carbs, 20g fat, 2g fiber.

5-Spice Tofu Scramble

Yields: 2 servings **Prep time:** 5 minutes **Total time:** 20 minutes **Equipment:** Wok, spatula.

Ingredients: 1 block (14oz) tofu, crumbled, 1 tbsp oil, 1/2 diced onion, 2 minced garlic, 1/2 tsp five-spice powder, 1/4 tsp turmeric powder, red pepper flakes, 1/2 cup chopped veggies, 2 green onions, soy sauce, sesame oil.

Instructions: 1. Crumble tofu. 2. Heat 1 tbsp oil in a wok over medium heat. 3. Cook onion until softened. 4. Add garlic, spices, and flakes. 5. Cook for 30 sec or until fragrant. 6. Add the crumbled tofu to the wok and scramble it with a spatula. 7. Cook for 5-7 min or until the tofu is browned and heated through. 8. Stir in the mixed veggies and sliced green onions. 9. Cook for 2-3 min or until the veggies are crisp-tender. 10. Season with soy sauce and sesame oil. 11. Serve over rice or toast.

Nutritional info: 250 cal, 15g protein, 10g carbs, 15g fat, 3g fiber.

Sesame Beef Strips

Yields: 4 servings **Prep time:** 15 minutes **Total time:** 25 minutes **Equipment:** Wok, spatula.

Ingredients: 1 lb flank/sirloin, 1 tbsp soy sauce, cornstarch, sesame oil, 1/2 tsp ginger, pepper, 2 tbsp oil, 3 minced garlic cloves, 1 red & green bell pepper, 1/2 cup water chestnuts, 1/4 cup soy sauce, 2 tbsp honey, 1 tbsp rice vinegar, sesame oil, 1/4 tsp flakes, 1 tbsp sesame seeds.

Instructions: 1. Marinate beef in soy sauce, cornstarch, sesame oil, ginger, and pepper for at least 15 min. 2. Stir-fry in 1 tbsp hot oil for 3-4 min or until browned and cooked through. 3. Remove. 4. Add remaining oil, garlic, peppers, and water chestnuts (opt). 5. Stir-fry for 2-3 min. 6. Add soy sauce, honey, vinegar, sesame oil, and flakes. 7. Stir to combine. 8. Return the cooked beef to the wok and toss to coat with the sauce. 9. Cook for 1-2 min or until heated through. 10. Garnish with sesame seeds. 11. Serve.

Nutritional info: 400 cal, 25g protein, 25g carbs, 20g fat, 2g fiber.

Coconut Curry Shrimp

Yields: 2 servings **Prep time:** 10 minutes **Total time:** 25 minutes **Equipment:** Wok, spatula.

Ingredients: 1 lb shrimp, 1 tbsp oil, 1 diced onion, 2 minced garlic cloves, 1 tbsp red curry paste, 1 can coconut milk, 1/2 cup chopped bell pepper, broccoli florets, 1/4 cup cilantro, lime juice, salt, pepper.

Instructions: 1. Prep veggies. 2. Stir-fry shrimp in hot oil until pink. 3. Remove. 4. Fry onion and garlic for 2-3 min or until softened. 5. Add curry paste and cook for 30 sec or until fragrant. 6. Pour in the coconut milk and bring to a simmer. 7. Let simmer for 2-3 min or until the sauce has thickened slightly. 8. Add pepper and broccoli, and cook for 3-4 min or until the veggies are crisp-tender. 9. Return shrimp and cook for 1-2 min or until heated through. 10. Add cilantro. 11. Season with lime juice, salt, and pepper. 12. Serve.

Nutritional info: 400 cal, 30g protein, 20g carbs, 25g fat, 4g fiber.

Maple Ginger Tempeh

Yields: 4 servings **Prep time:** 10 minutes **Total time:** 25 minutes **Equipment:** Wok, spatula.

Ingredients: 8oz tempeh, cubed, 2 tbsp soy sauce, 2 tbsp maple syrup, 1 tbsp vinegar, 1 tsp ginger, 1/2 tsp garlic powder, 2 tbsp oil, 1 diced onion, 2 minced garlic, 1 diced red bell pepper, 1/2 cup broccoli florets, 1/4 cup water/broth, 1 tbsp cornstarch, 2 tbsp water, sesame seeds, green onions.

Instructions: 1. Marinate tempeh in soy sauce, maple syrup, vinegar, ginger, garlic powder for at least 15 min. 2. Stir-fry in hot oil for 3-4 min or until browned. 3. Remove. 4. Fry the diced onion, minced garlic, and red bell pepper for 2-3 min or until softened. 5. Add broccoli. 6. Stir in the broccoli florets and cook for 2-3 min or until crisp-tender. 7. Stir in water/broth mixed with cornstarch until thickened. 8. Return tempeh. 9. Cook for 1-2 min. 10. Garnish with sesame seeds and sliced green onions. 11. Serve.

Nutritional info: 350 cal, 20g protein, 30g carbs, 15g fat, 5g fiber.

Orange Glazed Chicken

Yields: 4 servings **Prep time:** 15 minutes **Total time:** 35 minutes **Equipment:** Wok, spatula.

Ingredients: 1 lb boneless chicken, 1 tbsp soy sauce, cornstarch, sesame oil, white pepper, 2 tbsp oil, 1 garlic clove, 1 tbsp ginger, 1/2 red & green bell pepper, 1/4 cup green onions, 1/2 cup orange juice, 1/4 cup soy sauce, 2 tbsp vinegar, 1 tbsp honey, 1 tbsp cornstarch, red pepper flakes, orange zest.

Instructions: 1. Marinate chicken for at least 15 min. 2. Whisk together the orange juice, soy sauce, rice vinegar, honey, cornstarch, and red pepper flakes. 3. Heat 1 tbsp oil in a wok over high heat. 4. Add the marinated chicken and stir-fry for 3-4 min or until cooked through and browned. 5. Remove the chicken from the wok and set aside. 6. Stir-fry garlic, ginger, and white onions for 30 sec or until fragrant. 7. Add peppers. 8. Cook for 2-3 min or until crisp-tender. 9. Return chicken and add glaze. 10. Cook until thickened. 11. Garnish with zest, onions. 12. Serve.

Nutritional info: 350 cal, 25g protein, 30g carbs, 10g fat, 2g fiber.

Pineapple Pork Stir-fry

Yields: 4 servings **Prep time:** 15 minutes **Total time:** 30 minutes **Equipment:** Wok, spatula.

Ingredients: 1 lb pork loin, 1 tbsp soy sauce, cornstarch, sesame oil, 1/2 tsp ginger, 2 tbsp oil, 1 red & green bell pepper, 1/2 onion, 1 can pineapple chunks, 1/4 cup reserved juice & soy sauce, 2 tbsp rice vinegar, 1 tbsp honey, 1 tbsp cornstarch, 1/4 tsp red pepper flakes, sesame seeds, green onions.

Instructions: 1. Marinate pork in soy sauce, cornstarch, sesame oil, and ginger for 15 min. 2. Heat 1 tbsp oil in a wok over high heat. 3. Add the marinated pork and stir-fry for 3-4 min. 4. Remove the pork from the wok and set aside. 5. Add the remaining 1 tbsp oil to the wok, and stir-fry the peppers and onion for 2-3 min. 6. Pour the pineapple juice, soy sauce, rice vinegar, honey, and red pepper flakes over the veggies. 7. Stir, whisk together the cornstarch with 2 tbsp water, add the cornstarch slurry to the wok. 8. Cook for 1 min. 9. Return the cooked pork and pineapple chunks to the wok, toss to coat with the sauce. 10. Cook for 1-2 min. 11. Garnish, serve.

Nutritional info: 400 cal, 25g protein, 35g carbs, 15g fat, 2g fiber.

Spicy Chili Garlic Noodles

Yields: 2 servings **Prep time:** 5 minutes **Total time:** 15 minutes **Equipment:** Wok, spatula.

Ingredients: 8oz noodles, 2 tbsp oil, 4 minced garlic cloves, 1 tbsp chili garlic sauce, 1/4 cup soy sauce, 1 tbsp rice vinegar, 1 tsp sugar, 1/4 cup chopped green onions, cilantro, sesame seeds.

Instructions: 1. Cook noodles. 2. Heat 2 tbsp oil in a wok over high heat. 3. Add the minced garlic and stir-fry for 30 sec. 4. Stir in the chili garlic sauce and cook for an extra 30 sec. 5. Add soy sauce, vinegar, and sugar. 6. Add noodles and toss. 7. Cook for 1-2 min. 8. Garnish with onions, cilantro, seeds. 9. Serve.

Nutritional info: 400 cal, 10g protein, 55g carbs, 15g fat, 2g fiber.

Green Bean & Almond Stir-fry

Yields: 4 servings **Prep time:** 5 minutes **Total time:** 15 minutes **Equipment:** Wok, spatula.

Ingredients: 1 lb green beans, 2 tbsp oil, 2 minced garlic cloves, 1 tbsp ginger, 1/4 cup almonds, 2 tbsp soy sauce, 1 tbsp oyster sauce, 1 tsp sesame oil, red pepper flakes.

Instructions: 1. (Opt) Blanch beans in boiling water, drain, and rinse. 2. Heat 2 tbsp oil in a wok over high heat. 3. Stir-fry garlic and ginger for 30 sec or until fragrant. 4. Add almonds and stir-fry until toasted. 5. Add beans and cook until tender-crisp. 6. Add sauces, oil, and flakes. 7. Cook for 1 min. 8. Serve.

Nutritional info: 200 cal, 5g protein, 10g carbs, 15g fat, 4g fiber.

Easy Stir-fries

Egg Fried Rice Express

Yields: 2 servings **Prep time:** 5 minutes **Total time:** 15 minutes **Equipment:** Wok, spatula.

Ingredients: 2 cups cooked rice, 2 tbsp oil, 2 eggs, 2 garlic cloves, 1/2 cup peas & carrots, 1/4 cup diced onion & green pepper, 2 green onions, 2 tbsp soy sauce, 1 tsp sesame oil, salt, pepper.

Instructions: 1. Scramble eggs in 1 tbsp hot oil. 2. Remove. 3. Stir-fry garlic, onion, and pepper for 2-3 min. 4. Add peas & carrots. 5. Cook for 2-3 min or until heated through and slightly softened. 6. Add rice, soy sauce, sesame oil, salt, and pepper. 7. Return eggs and green onions. 8. Heat through. 9. Garnish with sliced green onions. 10. Serve hot.

Nutritional info: 400 cal, 10g protein, 55g carbs, 15g fat, 2g fiber.

Speedy Sesame Chicken

Yields: 4 servings **Prep time:** 10 minutes **Total time:** 25 minutes **Equipment:** Wok, spatula.

Ingredients: 1 lb boneless chicken, 1 tbsp soy sauce, cornstarch, sesame oil, 1/4 tsp white pepper, 2 tbsp oil, 1 garlic clove, 1 tbsp ginger, 1/2 red & green bell pepper, 1/4 cup green onions (white/green separated), 1/4 cup soy sauce, 2 tbsp honey, 1 tbsp rice vinegar, sesame oil, 1 tsp cornstarch, 1/4 cup water, sesame seeds.

Instructions: 1. Marinate chicken for at least 15 min. 2. Whisk sauce ingredients. 3. Stir-fry chicken in 1 tbsp hot oil until cooked. 4. Remove. 5. Stir-fry garlic, ginger, and white onions for 30 sec or until fragrant. 6. Add peppers. 7. Cook for 2-3 min or until crisp-tender. 8. Return chicken and add sauce. 9. Cook until thickened. 10. Garnish with seeds and onions. 11. Serve.

Nutritional info: 400 cal, 25g protein, 30g carbs, 15g fat, 2g fiber.

Garlic Shrimp Stir-fry

Yields: 2 servings **Prep time:** 10 minutes **Total time:** 20 minutes **Equipment:** Wok, spatula.

Ingredients: 1 lb shrimp, 1 tsp cornstarch, 1/2 tsp salt, 1/4 tsp pepper, 2 tbsp oil, 5-6 minced garlic cloves, 1 tbsp ginger, 1 sliced red bell pepper, 1 cup broccoli florets, 1/4 cup water/broth, 1 tbsp soy sauce, 1 tsp sesame oil, 1/2 tsp sugar, red pepper flakes, green onions, sesame seeds.

Instructions: 1. Toss shrimp with cornstarch, salt, and pepper. 2. Heat 2 tbsp oil in a wok over high heat. 3. Add the marinated shrimp and stir-fry for 2-3 min or until pink and cooked through. 4. Remove. 5. Fry garlic and ginger for 30 sec or until fragrant. 6. Add pepper and broccoli and cook until tender. 7. Add water/broth, soy sauce, sesame oil, sugar, flakes. 8. Return shrimp and cook. 9. Cook for 1-2 min or until heated through. 10. Garnish with sliced green onions and sesame seeds. 11. Serve.

Nutritional info: 350 cal, 25g protein, 20g carbs, 18g fat, 2g fiber.

15-Minute Beef & Broccoli

Yields: 2 servings **Prep time:** 5 minutes **Total time:** 15 minutes **Equipment:** Wok, spatula.

Ingredients: 1/2 lb flank/sirloin, 1 tbsp soy sauce, 1 tsp cornstarch, 1/2 tsp sesame oil, 1 tbsp oil, 3 minced garlic, 1 tbsp ginger, 2 cups broccoli, 1/4 cup water/broth, 2 tbsp oyster sauce, 1 tbsp soy sauce, 1 tsp sugar, red pepper flakes.

Instructions: 1. Marinate beef in soy sauce, cornstarch, and sesame oil for at least 10 min. 2. Heat 1 tbsp oil in a wok over high heat. 3. Add the marinated beef and stir-fry for 2-3 min or until browned and cooked through. 4. Remove. 5. Fry garlic and ginger for 30 sec or until fragrant. 6. Add broccoli and cook for 2-3 min. 7. Add water/broth, oyster sauce, soy sauce, sugar, flakes. 8. Bring the sauce to a simmer and cook for 1-2 min or until slightly thickened. 9. Return beef and cook 1-2 min. 10. Serve over rice/noodles.

Nutritional info: 350 cal, 25g protein, 20g carbs, 18g fat, 4g fiber.

Teriyaki Tofu Blitz

Yields: 2 servings **Prep time:** 10 minutes **Total time:** 25 minutes **Equipment:** Wok, spatula.

Ingredients: 1 block (14oz) tofu, cubed, 1 tbsp cornstarch, 2 tbsp oil, 1/2 cup chopped broccoli, sliced carrots, 1/4 cup sliced red bell pepper, 2 green onions, 1/4 cup soy sauce, 2 tbsp mirin, 1 tbsp honey/maple syrup, 1 tsp ginger, 1/2 tsp garlic powder.

Instructions: 1. Coat tofu in cornstarch, fry in 1 tbsp hot oil until golden. 2. Remove. 3. Stir-fry broccoli, carrots, and pepper in remaining oil. 4. Whisk sauce ingredients and add to wok. 5. Return tofu and add white onions. 6. Cook for 1-2 min. 7. Garnish with green onions. 8. Serve.

Nutritional info: 350 cal, 20g protein, 30g carbs, 15g fat, 5g fiber.

Quick Spicy Peanut Noodles

Yields: 2 servings **Prep time:** 5 minutes **Total time:** 15 minutes **Equipment:** Wok, spatula.

Ingredients: 8oz rice noodles, 1 tbsp oil, 2 minced garlic cloves, 1 tbsp ginger, 1/4 cup peanut butter, 2 tbsp soy sauce, 1 tbsp rice vinegar, 1 tbsp honey/syrup, 1-2 tsp chili garlic sauce, 1/4 cup chopped green onions & peanuts, 1/2 cup carrots, 1/2 cup cucumber, 1/4 cup bean sprouts.

Instructions: 1. Cook noodles. 2. Whisk peanut butter, soy sauce, vinegar, sweetener, and chili garlic sauce. 3. Stir-fry garlic and ginger in hot oil. 4. (Opt) Add carrots, cucumber, and bean sprouts. 5. Add sauce and heat. 6. Add noodles and toss. 6. Garnish with onions and peanuts. 7. Serve.

Nutritional info: 450 cal, 12g protein, 60g carbs, 20g fat, 4g fiber.

Vegetable Lo Mein in a Flash

Yields: 2 servings **Prep time:** 10 minutes **Total time:** 25 minutes **Equipment:** Wok, spatula.

Ingredients: 6oz lo mein noodles, 1 tbsp oil, 2 minced garlic cloves, 1 tbsp ginger, 1/2 cup sliced carrots, broccoli florets, mushrooms, 1/4 cup snow peas, 2 green onions (white/green separated), 1/4 cup soy sauce, 1 tbsp oyster sauce, 1 tsp sesame oil, 1 tsp sugar, red pepper flakes.

Instructions: 1. Cook/prep noodles. 2. Whisk together the peanut butter, soy sauce, rice vinegar, honey or maple syrup, and chili garlic sauce. 3. Adjust the amount of chili garlic sauce to your desired level of spiciness. 4. Heat 1 tbsp oil in a wok over high heat. 5. Stir-fry garlic and ginger in hot oil for 30 sec or until fragrant. 6. Add carrots, broccoli, and mushrooms and stir-fry for 2-3 min or until slightly softened. 7. Add snow peas and white onions. 8. Stir-fry for 2-3 min or until slightly softened. 9. Add noodles and sauce. 10. Cook for 1-2 min. 11. Garnish with green onions. 12. Serve.

Nutritional info: 400 cal, 10g protein, 55g carbs, 15g fat, 4g fiber.

Honey Garlic Pork Stir-fry

Yields: 4 servings **Prep time:** 10 minutes **Total time:** 25 minutes **Equipment:** Wok, spatula.

Ingredients: 1 lb pork loin, 1 tbsp soy sauce, cornstarch, sesame oil, 1/4 tsp pepper, 2 tbsp oil, 5-6 minced garlic cloves, 1 tbsp ginger, 1 red & green bell pepper, 1/2 onion, 1/4 cup water/broth, 1/4 cup honey, 2 tbsp soy sauce, 1 tbsp vinegar, 1 tsp cornstarch, 1/4 cup water, sesame seeds, green onions.

Instructions: 1. Marinate pork in soy sauce, cornstarch, sesame oil, and pepper for at least 15 min. 2. Heat 1 tbsp oil in a wok over high heat. 3. Add the marinated pork and stir-fry for 3-4 min or until browned and cooked through. 4. Remove. 5. Stir-fry garlic and ginger for 30 sec or until fragrant. 6. Add peppers and onion. 7. Cook for 2-3 min or until crisp-tender. 8. Whisk honey, soy sauce, vinegar, cornstarch, 1/4 cup water. 9. Add to wok, simmer, and cook for 1-2 min or until the sauce has thickened. 10. Return pork and add water/broth. 11. Cook for 1-2 min or until heated through. 12. Garnish and serve.

Nutritional info: 400 cal, 25g protein, 35g carbs, 15g fat, 2g fiber.

Thai Basil Chicken Express

Yields: 2 servings **Prep time:** 10 minutes **Total time:** 25 minutes **Equipment:** Wok, spatula.

Ingredients: 1 lb boneless chicken, 2 tbsp oil, 4-6 garlic cloves, 2-4 Thai chilies, 1/2 onion, 1 red bell pepper, 1/2 cup green beans, 2 tbsp soy sauce, 1 tbsp fish & oyster sauce, 1 tbsp brown sugar, 1/4 cup water, 2 cups Thai basil leaves, jasmine rice.

Instructions: 1. Prep veggies and combine sauce ingredients. 2. Heat 2 tbsp oil in a wok over high heat. 3. Add the chicken and stir-fry for 3-4 min or until cooked through and browned. 4. Remove the chicken from the wok and set aside. 5. Add garlic and chilies. 6. Stir-fry for 30 sec or until fragrant. 7. Add onion, pepper, and beans. 8. Cook for 3-4 min or until the veggies are crisp-tender. 9. Add sauce and cook until thickened. 10. Stir in the Thai basil leaves. 11. Cook for 30 sec or just until the basil wilts slightly. 12. Serve over jasmine rice.

Nutritional info: 450 cal, 30g protein, 40g carbs, 20g fat, 4g fiber.

Super Simple Shrimp & Snow Peas

Yields: 2 servings **Prep time:** 5 minutes **Total time:** 15 minutes **Equipment:** Wok, spatula.

Ingredients: 1 lb shrimp, 1 tbsp cornstarch, 1 tbsp oil, 2 minced garlic, 1-inch ginger, 6oz snow peas, 2 tbsp soy sauce, 1 tbsp oyster sauce, 1/4 cup water/broth, 1 tsp sesame oil, red pepper flakes, sesame seeds, green onions.

Instructions: 1. Coat shrimp in cornstarch. 2. Heat 1 tbsp oil in a wok over high heat. 3. Add the marinated shrimp and stir-fry for 2-3 min or until pink and cooked through. 4. Remove. 5. Fry garlic and ginger for 30 sec or until fragrant. 6. Add snow peas. 7. Stir-fry for 1-2 min or until crisp-tender. 8. Add sauces, water/broth, oil, flakes. 9. Return shrimp. 10. Cook for 1-2 min or until heated through. 11. Garnish with sliced green onions and sesame seeds. 12. Serve.

Nutritional info: 300 cal, 25g protein, 15g carbs, 15g fat, 2g fiber.

Lemon Pepper Tofu Scramble

Yields: 2 servings **Prep time:** 5 minutes **Total time:** 20 minutes **Equipment:** Wok, spatula.

Ingredients: 1 block (14oz) tofu, crumbled, 1 tbsp olive oil, 1/2 diced onion, 2 minced garlic, 1/2 tsp lemon pepper, 1/4 tsp turmeric powder (optional), 1/4 cup parsley, dill, 1/2 lemon juice, salt, pepper, 1/2 cup chopped bell pepper, mushrooms, 1/4 cup spinach (all optional).

Instructions: 1. Crumble tofu. 2. Heat 1 tbsp olive oil in a wok over medium heat. 3. Add the diced onion and cook for 2-3 min or until softened. 4. Stir in the minced garlic, lemon pepper seasoning, and turmeric powder (opt). 5. Cook for 30 sec or until fragrant. 6. Add the crumbled tofu to the wok and scramble it with a spatula. 7. Cook for 5-7 min or until the tofu is browned and heated through. 8. Add the chopped bell pepper, mushrooms, and spinach to the wok (opt). 9. Cook for 2-3 min or until the veggies are tender-crisp. 10. Stir in the chopped parsley, dill, lemon juice, salt, and pepper. 11. Cook for 1 min or until the flavors are combined. 12. Serve.

Nutritional info: 280 cal, 18g protein, 10g carbs, 18g fat, 3g fiber.

Chapter 4: Stir-Fries Magic

Vegetable Stir-Fries

Rainbow Veggie Medley

Yields: 4 servings **Prep time:** 10 minutes **Total time:** 25 minutes **Equipment:** Wok, spatula.

Ingredients: 1 tbsp oil, 1 red, orange, yellow bell pepper, 1/2 red onion, 1 cup broccoli florets, 1 cup snap/snow peas, 2 minced garlic, 1 tbsp ginger, 1/4 cup soy sauce, 1 tbsp vinegar, 1 tsp sesame oil, flakes (optional), sesame seeds.

Instructions: 1. Slice veggies. 2. Mix soy sauce, vinegar, sesame oil, and flakes. 3. Heat 1 tbsp oil in a wok over high heat. 4. Add the minced garlic and grated ginger and stir-fry for 30 sec or until fragrant. 5. Add onion, peppers and stir-fry. 6. Add broccoli and peas. 7. Stir-fry for 5-7 min or until the veggies are crisp-tender. 8. Add sauce. 9. Cook for 1 min. 10. Garnish with seeds. 11. Serve.

Nutritional info: 200 cal, 5g protein, 25g carbs, 10g fat, 5g fiber.

Garlic Ginger Broccoli

Yields: 4 servings **Prep time:** 5 minutes **Total time:** 15 minutes **Equipment:** Wok, spatula.

Ingredients: 1 large head of broccoli, 2 tbsp oil, 4 minced garlic cloves, 1 tbsp ginger, 2 tbsp soy sauce, 1 tbsp oyster sauce (optional), 1/2 tsp sesame oil, red pepper flakes, sesame seeds.

Instructions: 1. Blanch broccoli in salted water, drain, and rinse. 2. Heat 2 tbsp oil in a wok. 3. Stir-fry garlic and ginger for 30 sec or until fragrant. 4. Add broccoli, cook 2-3 min. 5. Drizzle with sauces, sesame oil, flakes. 6. Toss. 7. Garnish with seeds. 8. Serve.

Nutritional info: 100 cal, 5g protein, 8g carbs, 7g fat, 4g fiber.

Spicy Szechuan Green Beans

Yields: 4 servings **Prep time:** 5 minutes **Total time:** 20 minutes **Equipment:** Wok, spatula.

Ingredients: 1 lb green beans, 1 tbsp oil, 2 minced garlic cloves, 1 tbsp ginger, 1 tbsp Sichuan peppercorns, 3-4 dried chilies, 1/4 cup rice wine, 2 tbsp soy sauce, 1 tbsp black vinegar, 1 tsp sugar, 1/4 tsp sesame oil, sesame seeds.

Instructions: 1. Toast peppercorns and grind. 2. Stir-fry beans in hot oil until blistered. 3. Remove. 4. Fry garlic, ginger, chilies, and peppercorns for 30 sec or until fragrant. 5. Add rice wine, deglaze wok. 6. Add soy sauce, vinegar, sugar. 7. Bring to a simmer and cook for 1 min or until the sauce has thickened slightly. 8. Return beans and drizzle sesame oil. 9. Toss. 10. Garnish. 11. Serve.

Nutritional info: 150 cal, 4g protein, 12g carbs, 10g fat, 4g fiber.

Kung Pao Brussels Sprouts

Yields: 4 servings **Prep time:** 10 minutes **Total time:** 25 minutes **Equipment:** Wok, spatula.

Ingredients: 1 lb Brussels sprouts, 1 tbsp oil, 1/4 cup peanuts, 8-10 dried chilies, 3 minced garlic cloves, 1 tbsp ginger, 1/4 cup soy sauce, 2 tbsp vinegar, 1 tbsp rice wine, 1 tbsp honey, 1 tsp cornstarch, 1/4 cup water.

Instructions: 1. Whisk together the soy sauce, rice vinegar, honey, cornstarch, and water. 2. Fry peanuts in 1/2 tbsp hot oil until toasted. 3. Remove. 4. Add the remaining 1/2 tbsp oil to the wok. 5. Stir-fry the Brussels sprouts for 3-4 min or until crisp-tender. 6. Push the Brussels sprouts to one side of the wok. 7. Add the minced garlic, grated ginger, and dried red chilies. 8. Stir-fry for 30 sec or until fragrant. 9. Pour the prepared sauce over the veggies and bring to a simmer. 10. Cook for 2-3 min or until the sauce has thickened. 11. Return sprouts and add sauce. 12. Cook until thickened. 13. Add the toasted peanuts and toss to combine. 14. Serve.

Nutritional info: 200 cal, 5g protein, 15g carbs, 12g fat, 4g fiber.

Sweet & Sour Cauliflower

Yields: 4 servings **Prep time:** 10 minutes **Total time:** 25 minutes **Equipment:** Wok, spatula.

Ingredients: 1 head cauliflower, 1/4 cup cornstarch, 1/2 tsp salt, pepper, 2 tbsp oil, 1/2 diced onion, 1 red & green bell pepper, 1 can pineapple chunks, 1/2 cup juice, 1/4 cup vinegar, 2 tbsp ketchup & soy sauce, 1 tbsp sugar & cornstarch, red pepper flakes.

Instructions: 1. Coat cauliflower, fry in 1 tbsp hot oil until tender-crisp. 2. Remove. 3. Fry onion and peppers for 2-3 min or until softened. 4. Add juice, vinegar, sauces, sugar, flakes. 5. Whisk together the 1 tbsp cornstarch with 2 tbsp water. 6. Add the cornstarch slurry to the wok and cook for 1 min or until the sauce has thickened. 7. Return cauliflower, pineapple. 8. Cook for 1 min. 9. Serve over rice/quinoa.

Nutritional info: 250 cal, 5g protein, 35g carbs, 10g fat, 4g fiber.

Broccoli & Cashew Stir-fry

Yields: 4 servings **Prep time:** 10 minutes **Total time:** 25 minutes **Equipment:** Wok, spatula.

Ingredients: 1 head broccoli, 1 tbsp oil, 3 minced garlic cloves, 1 tbsp ginger, 1/2 cup chopped onion, sliced carrots, 1/2 cup cashews, 1/4 cup water/broth, 2 tbsp soy sauce, 1 tbsp oyster sauce, 1 tsp sesame oil, 1 tsp sugar, red pepper flakes, 1 tbsp cornstarch, 2 tbsp water.

Instructions: 1. Bring a large pot of salted water to a boil. 2. Add the broccoli florets and blanch for 1-2 min or until bright green. 3. Drain and rinse with cold water to stop the cooking process. 4. Whisk sauce ingredients (except slurry). 5. Stir-fry garlic, ginger, and onion in hot oil for 30 sec or until fragrant. 6. Add carrots, broccoli. 7. Stir-fry for 3-4 min or until the veggies are crisp-tender. 8. Pour sauce and thicken with slurry. 9. Bring to a simmer and cook for 1-2 min or until the sauce has thickened slightly. 10. Whisk together the cornstarch and water. 11. Add the cornstarch slurry to the wok and cook for 1 min or until the sauce has thickened further. 12. Stir in the cashews. 13. Cook for an extra 30 sec or until heated through. 14. Serve over rice/noodles.

Nutritional info: 250 cal, 8g protein, 20g carbs, 15g fat, 5g fiber.

Mushroom & Asparagus Delight

Yields: 4 servings **Prep time:** 10 minutes **Total time:** 25 minutes **Equipment:** Wok, spatula.

Ingredients: 1 lb asparagus, 8oz sliced mushrooms, 2 tbsp oil, 3 minced garlic cloves, 1 tbsp ginger, 1/4 cup soy sauce, 1 tbsp oyster sauce, 1 tsp sesame oil, 1/4 cup green onions, sesame seeds.

Instructions: 1. Wash & prep veggies. 2. Mix soy sauce, oyster sauce, sesame oil. 3. Heat 2 tbsp oil in a wok over high heat. 4. Add the sliced mushrooms and stir-fry for 3-4 min or until browned. 5. Add asparagus and cook until tender-crisp. 6. Push aside and fry garlic and ginger for 30 sec or until fragrant. 7. Add sauce mixture, onions. 8. Toss. 9. Garnish with sliced green onions and sesame seeds. 10. Serve.

Nutritional info: 200 cal, 8g protein, 15g carbs, 12g fat, 4g fiber.

Honey Glazed Carrots & Snow Peas

Yields: 4 servings **Prep time:** 5 minutes **Total time:** 15 minutes **Equipment:** Wok, spatula.

Ingredients: 4 carrots, 6oz snow peas, 1 tbsp oil, 2 minced garlic cloves, 1 tbsp ginger, 1/4 cup honey, 2 tbsp soy sauce, 1 tbsp rice vinegar, 1/4 tsp red pepper flakes, sesame seeds.

Instructions: 1. Heat 1 tbsp oil in a wok over high heat. 2. Add the sliced carrots and stir-fry for 3-4 min or until softened. 3. Add snow peas and cook until crisp-tender. 4. Add garlic and ginger. 5. Stir-fry for 30 sec or until fragrant. 6. Drizzle honey, soy sauce, vinegar. 7. Add flakes. 8. Cook for 1-2 min or until the sauce has thickened and glazed the veggies. 9. Garnish with sesame seeds. 10. Serve.

Nutritional info: 150 cal, 2g protein, 20g carbs, 7g fat, 3g fiber.

Spicy Eggplant Stir-fry

Yields: 4 servings **Prep time:** 10 minutes **Total time:** 25 minutes **Equipment:** Wok, spatula.

Ingredients: 1 large eggplant (cubed), 1 tbsp cornstarch, 2 tbsp oil, 3 minced garlic cloves, 1 tbsp ginger, 1/2 cup chopped green bell pepper, 1/4 cup chopped red onion, 2-3 Thai chilies (or 1/2 tsp red pepper flakes), 2 tbsp soy sauce, 1 tbsp oyster sauce, 1 tbsp rice wine, 1 tbsp brown sugar, 1 tsp sesame oil, 1/4 cup water, chopped green onions, cilantro.

Instructions: 1. Toss eggplant with cornstarch. 2. Heat 1 tbsp oil in a wok over high heat. 3. Add the marinated eggplant and stir-fry for 3-4 min per side or until golden brown. 4. Remove. 5. Add the remaining 1 tbsp oil to the wok. 6. Stir-fry the minced garlic, grated ginger, red bell pepper, green onion, and Thai chilies (or red pepper flakes) for 2-3 min or until fragrant. 7. Pour in the soy sauce, oyster sauce, rice wine, brown sugar, and water. 8. Stir to combine. 9. Return the cooked eggplant to the wok and toss to coat with the sauce. 10. Cook for 1-2 min or until heated through. 11. Garnish with chopped green onions and cilantro. 12. Serve

Nutritional info: 250 cal, 5g protein, 30g carbs, 12g fat, 4g fiber.

Pineapple & Veggie Stir-fry

Yields: 4 servings **Prep time:** 10 minutes **Total time:** 25 minutes **Equipment:** Wok, spatula.

Ingredients: 1 tbsp oil, 1 red & green bell pepper, 1/2 red onion, 1 cup broccoli, snap/snow peas, 1 can pineapple chunks (juice reserved), 2 minced garlic, 1 tbsp ginger, 1/4 cup reserved pineapple juice & soy sauce, 2 tbsp rice vinegar, 1 tbsp honey, 1 tsp cornstarch, 1/4 tsp red pepper flakes, sesame seeds, green onions.

Instructions: 1. Slice veggies. 2. Whisk together the soy sauce, rice vinegar, honey, cornstarch, and red pepper flakes. 3. Stir-fry garlic and ginger in hot oil for 30 sec or until fragrant. 4. Add onion, peppers, and stir-fry. 5. Add broccoli, peas, pineapple. 6. Stir-fry until tender. 7. Add sauce. 8. Cook for 1 min. 9. Garnish with seeds and onions. 10. Serve.

Nutritional info: 250 cal, 4g protein, 35g carbs, 10g fat, 5g fiber.

Tofu and Tempeh Stir-Fries

Sesame Ginger Tofu

Yields: 4 servings **Prep time:** 10 minutes **Total time:** 25 minutes **Equipment:** Wok, spatula.

Ingredients: 1 block (14oz) tofu, cubed, 2 tbsp cornstarch, 1/2 tsp salt, pepper, 2 tbsp oil, 1/2 sliced onion, 1 sliced red bell pepper, 1/2 cup broccoli florets, 2 minced garlic cloves, 1 tbsp ginger, 1/4 cup soy sauce, 2 tbsp rice vinegar, 1 tbsp honey/maple syrup, 1 tbsp sesame oil, 1 tsp cornstarch, 1/4 cup water, sesame seeds, green onions.

Instructions: 1. Coat tofu in cornstarch, salt, and pepper. 2. Fry in 1 tbsp hot oil until golden. 3. Remove. 4. Stir-fry onion, pepper, and broccoli in the remaining oil for 3-4 min or until crisp-tender. 5. Add garlic and ginger. 6. Add sauce ingredients (whisk soy sauce, vinegar, sweetener, oils, cornstarch, water). 7. Return tofu and cook until heated through. 8. Garnish with sesame seeds and sliced green onions. 9. Serve.

Nutritional info: 350 cal, 20g protein, 30g carbs, 15g fat, 4g fiber.

Kung Pao Tofu

Yields: 4 servings **Prep time:** 15 minutes **Total time:** 35 minutes **Equipment:** Wok, spatula.

Ingredients: 1 block (14oz) tofu, cubed, 2 tbsp cornstarch, 1/4 tsp salt, 2 tbsp oil, 1 tbsp Sichuan peppercorns, 8-10 dried chilies, 3 minced garlic, 1-inch ginger, 1/2 red & green bell pepper, 1/4 cup peanuts, 3 green onions, 2 tbsp soy sauce, 1 tbsp vinegar, 1 tbsp rice wine, 1 tbsp sugar, 1 tsp cornstarch, 1/4 cup water.

Instructions: 1. Coat tofu in cornstarch, salt. 2. Toast peppercorns, grind. 3. Mix sauce ingredients. 4. Stir-fry tofu in 1 tbsp hot oil until golden. 5. Remove. 6. Stir-fry chilies, garlic, ginger for 30 sec or until fragrant. 7. Add peppers. 8. Return tofu, add sauce, peppercorns. 9. Cook for 1 min. 10. Stir in peanuts and onions. 11. Serve.

Nutritional info: 400 cal, 18g protein, 35g carbs, 20g fat, 4g fiber.

Sweet & Sour Tofu

Yields: 4 servings **Prep time:** 10 minutes **Total time:** 25 minutes **Equipment:** Wok, spatula.

Ingredients: 1 block (14oz) tofu, cubed, 1/4 cup cornstarch, 1/2 tsp salt, pepper, 2 tbsp oil, 1/2 diced onion, 1 red & green bell pepper, 1 can pineapple chunks (juice reserved), 1/2 cup juice, 1/4 cup vinegar, 2 tbsp ketchup & soy sauce, 1 tbsp sugar & cornstarch, red pepper flakes.

Instructions: 1. Coat tofu in cornstarch, salt, and pepper. 2. Fry in 1 tbsp hot oil until golden. 3. Remove. 4. Stir-fry onion and peppers in the remaining oil for 2-3 min or until softened. 5. Add juice, vinegar, ketchup, soy sauce, sugar, flakes. 6. Whisk together the 1 tbsp cornstarch with 2 tbsp water. 7. Add the cornstarch slurry to the wok and cook for 1 min or until the sauce has thickened. 8. Return tofu, pineapple. 9. Cook for 1 min. 10. Serve over rice/noodles.

Nutritional info: 350 cal, 15g protein, 40g carbs, 12g fat, 4g fiber.

Spicy Peanut Tofu

Yields: 4 servings **Prep time:** 10 minutes **Total time:** 25 minutes **Equipment:** Wok, spatula.

Ingredients: 1 block (14oz) tofu, cubed, 1 tbsp cornstarch, salt, pepper, 2 tbsp oil, 1/2 cup chopped onion, 1 red bell pepper, 1/2 cup broccoli florets, 2 garlic cloves, 1 tbsp ginger, 1/4 cup peanuts, 1/4 cup peanut butter, soy sauce, 2 tbsp rice vinegar, 1 tbsp honey/syrup, 1-2 tbsp chili garlic sauce, 1/4 cup water, green onions/cilantro (optional).

Instructions: 1. Coat tofu in cornstarch, salt, and pepper. 2. Fry in 1 tbsp oil until golden. 3. Remove. 4. Stir-fry onion and pepper until softened. 5. Add broccoli, garlic, ginger. 6. Stir-fry for 30 sec or until fragrant. 7. Whisk together the peanut butter, soy sauce, rice vinegar, honey or maple syrup, chili garlic sauce, and water and add to the wok. 8. Return tofu, peanuts. 9. Toss. 10. Cook for 1-2 min or until heated through. 11. Garnish with chopped green onions or cilantro, and sprinkle with peanuts. 12. Serve over rice/noodles.

Nutritional info: 450 cal, 20g protein, 35g carbs, 25g fat, 5g fiber.

General Tso's Tofu

Yields: 4 servings **Prep time:** 15 minutes **Total time:** 35 minutes **Equipment:** Wok, spatula.

Ingredients: 1 block (14oz) tofu, cubed, 1/4 cup cornstarch, 1/2 tsp salt, pepper, 2 tbsp oil, 2 minced garlic, 1 tbsp ginger, 2 dried chilies (or 1/2 tsp flakes), green onions (separated), 1/4 cup soy sauce, 2 tbsp hoisin sauce, 1 tbsp rice vinegar, 1 tbsp cooking wine, 2 tbsp sugar, 1 tsp cornstarch, 1/4 cup water.

Instructions: 1. Coat tofu in cornstarch, salt, and pepper. 2. Fry in 1 tbsp hot oil until golden. 3. Remove. 4. Stir-fry garlic, ginger, and chilies in the remaining oil for 30 sec or until fragrant. 5. Add sauces, wine, sugar, water. 6. Thicken with cornstarch slurry (2 tbsp water). 7. Return tofu and white onions. 8. Cook for 1-2 min or until the sauce has thickened and coats the tofu. 9. Garnish with green onions. 10. Serve over rice/noodles.

Nutritional info: 400 cal, 20g protein, 40g carbs, 18g fat, 4g fiber.

Black Pepper Tofu & Broccoli

Yields: 4 servings **Prep time:** 10 minutes **Total time:** 25 minutes **Equipment:** Wok, spatula.

Ingredients: 1 block (14oz) tofu, cubed, 1 tbsp cornstarch, 1/2 tsp salt, pepper, 2 tbsp oil, 3 minced garlic cloves, 1 tbsp ginger, 2 cups broccoli florets, 1/4 cup water/broth, 2 tbsp soy sauce, 1 tbsp oyster sauce, 1 tsp sugar, 1 tsp black pepper.

Instructions: 1. Coat tofu in cornstarch, salt, and pepper. 2. Heat 1 tbsp oil in a wok over high heat. 3. Add the marinated tofu and stir-fry for 3-4 min per side or until golden brown. 4. Remove. 5. Stir-fry garlic and ginger for 30 sec or until fragrant. 6. Add broccoli and cook for 2-3 min or until crisp-tender. 7. Add water/broth, sauces, sugar, and pepper. 8. Return tofu. 9. Cook for 1-2 min or until heated through. 10. Serve.

Nutritional info: 300 cal, 18g protein, 20g carbs, 15g fat, 4g fiber.

Teriyaki Tempeh

Yields: 4 servings **Prep time:** 10 minutes **Total time:** 25 minutes **Equipment:** Wok, spatula.

Ingredients: 8oz tempeh, 1 tbsp soy sauce & cornstarch, 2 tbsp oil, 1/2 onion, 1 bell pepper, 1/2 cup broccoli, 2 garlic cloves, 1 tbsp ginger, 1/4 cup soy sauce, 2 tbsp mirin, 1 tbsp honey/maple syrup, 1 tsp sesame oil, sesame seeds, green onions.

Instructions: 1. (Opt) Steam tempeh for 5-7 min to soften it before marinating. 2. Marinate in soy sauce & cornstarch for at least 10 min. 3. Heat 1 tbsp oil in a wok over high heat. 4. Add the marinated tempeh and stir-fry for 3-4 min per side or until golden brown. 5. Remove. 6. Stir-fry onion, pepper, and broccoli for 3-4 min or until crisp-tender. 7. Add garlic and ginger. 8. Cook for 30 sec or until fragrant. 9. Pour in the soy sauce, mirin, honey or maple syrup, and sesame oil. 10. Bring to a simmer and cook for 1-2 min or until the sauce has thickened slightly. 11. Return tempeh. 12. Cook for 1-2 min or until heated through. 13. Garnish with sesame seeds and sliced green onions. 14. Serve.

Nutritional info: 350 cal, 20g protein, 35g carbs, 15g fat, 5g fiber.

Orange Glazed Tempeh

Yields: 4 servings **Prep time:** 10 minutes **Total time:** 25 minutes **Equipment:** Wok, spatula.

Ingredients: 8 oz tempeh (cubed), 1 tbsp cornstarch, 2 tbsp oil, 1/2 onion (diced), 1 red bell pepper (diced), 1/2 cup broccoli florets, 2 garlic cloves (minced), 1 tbsp ginger, 1/2 cup orange juice, 2 tbsp soy sauce, 1 tbsp vinegar, 1 tbsp honey/maple syrup, 1 tsp cornstarch, 1/4 tsp red pepper flakes, orange zest.

Instructions: 1. Coat tempeh in cornstarch: combine the cornstarch, salt, and pepper (if using). 2. Add the cubed tempeh and toss to coat. 3. Heat 1 tbsp oil in a wok over high heat. 4. Add the marinated tempeh and stir-fry for 3-4 min per side or until golden brown. 5. Remove. 6. Stir-fry onion, pepper, and broccoli for 2-3 min or until crisp-tender. 7. Add garlic and ginger. 8. Cook for 30 sec or until fragrant. 9. Add orange glaze (mix juice, soy sauce, vinegar, sweetener, cornstarch, flakes). 10. Return tempeh. 11. Cook for 1-2 min or until heated through. 12. Garnish with orange zest, serve.

Nutritional info: 350 cal, 20g protein, 35g carbs, 15g fat, 5g fiber.

Spicy Tempeh & Green Beans

Yields: 4 servings **Prep time:** 10 minutes **Total time:** 25 minutes **Equipment:** Wok, spatula.

Ingredients: 8oz tempeh, 1 tbsp cornstarch, 2 tbsp oil, 1 diced onion, 3 minced garlic cloves, 1 tbsp ginger, 1 lb green beans, 1 red chili (optional), 1/4 cup soy sauce, 2 tbsp chili garlic sauce, 1 tbsp rice vinegar, 1 tbsp honey/maple syrup, 1/4 cup water.

Instructions: 1. Coat tempeh in cornstarch: combine the cornstarch, salt, and pepper (if using). 2. Add the cubed tempeh and toss to coat. 3. Heat 1 tbsp oil in a wok over high heat. 4. Add the marinated tempeh and stir-fry for 3-4 min per side or until golden brown. 5. Remove. 6. Stir-fry onion, garlic, ginger, and chili for 30 sec or until fragrant. 7. Add green beans and cook for 3-4 min or until crisp-tender. 8. Pour in the soy sauce, chili garlic sauce, rice vinegar, honey or maple syrup, and water. 9. Stir to combine. 10. Return tempeh and toss. 11. Cook for 1-2 min or until heated through. 12. Serve.

Nutritional info: 350 cal, 20g protein, 30g carbs, 18g fat, 5g fiber.

Coconut Curry Tempeh

Yields: 4 servings **Prep time:** 10 minutes **Total time:** 30 minutes **Equipment:** Wok, spatula.

Ingredients: 8oz tempeh, cubed, 1 tbsp oil, 1 diced onion, 2 minced garlic, 1 tbsp red curry paste, 1 can coconut milk, 1/2 cup chopped bell pepper, broccoli florets, 1/4 cup snow peas & chopped cilantro, 1 tbsp soy sauce, 1 tbsp lime juice, salt, pepper.

Instructions: 1. Chop veggies and mince garlic. 2. Heat 1 tbsp oil in a wok over high heat. 3. Add the cubed tempeh and stir-fry for 3-4 min per side or until golden brown. 4. Remove. 5. Fry onion and garlic for 2-3 min or until softened. 6. Add curry paste. 7. Cook for 30 sec or until fragrant. 8. Pour in the coconut milk and bring to a simmer. 9. Simmer for 2-3 min or until the sauce has thickened slightly. 10. Add pepper, broccoli and peas. 11. Cook for 3-4 min or until the veggies are crisp-tender. 12. Return tempeh. 13. Cook for 1-2 min or until heated through. 14. Add soy sauce, lime juice, salt, and pepper. 15. Garnish with cilantro. 16. Serve.

Nutritional info: 400 cal, 18g protein, 35g carbs, 22g fat, 5g fiber.

Tempeh Stir-fry with Cashews

Yields: 4 servings **Prep time:** 10 minutes **Total time:** 25 minutes **Equipment:** Wok, spatula.

Ingredients: 8oz tempeh, cubed, 2 tbsp soy sauce, 1 tbsp cornstarch, 1/2 tsp sesame oil, 2 tbsp oil, 1 diced onion, 1 diced red bell pepper, 1/2 cup broccoli florets, 2 minced garlic, 1 tbsp ginger, 1/2 cup cashews, 1/4 cup soy sauce, 1 tbsp hoisin sauce, 1 tbsp rice vinegar, 1 tbsp honey/maple syrup, 1 tsp cornstarch, 1/4 cup water, green onions, sesame seeds.

Instructions: 1. Marinate tempeh for at least 15 min. 2. Whisk sauce ingredients. 3. Fry tempeh in 1 tbsp hot oil until golden. 4. Remove. 5. Stir-fry onion, pepper, and broccoli in the remaining oil. 6. Add garlic and ginger. 7. Add sauce and simmer until thickened. 8. Return tempeh, cashews. 9. Cook for 1-2 min. 10. Garnish, serve.

Nutritional info: 400 cal, 18g protein, 35g carbs, 20g fat, 5g fiber.

Chicken Stir-Fries

Cashew Chicken

Yields: 4 servings **Prep time:** 15 minutes **Total time:** 30 minutes **Equipment:** Wok, spatula.

Ingredients: 1 lb boneless chicken, 1 tbsp soy sauce, cornstarch, sesame oil, 1/4 tsp pepper, 2 tbsp oil, 1/2 onion, 1 red & green bell pepper, 1/4 cup water chestnuts, 2 minced garlic cloves, 1 tbsp ginger, 1/2 cup cashews, 1/4 cup broth, 2 tbsp soy sauce, 1 tbsp oyster sauce, 1 tbsp honey/syrup, 1 tsp cornstarch, 1/4 cup water, green onions/cilantro.

Instructions: 1. Marinate chicken for at least 15 min. 2. Whisk together the soy sauce, oyster sauce, honey or maple syrup, cornstarch, and water. 3. Stir-fry chicken in 1 tbsp hot oil for 3-4 min. 4. Remove. 5. Stir-fry onion, peppers, and water chestnuts for 2-3 min or until crisp-tender. 6. Add garlic and ginger and cook for 30 sec or until fragrant. 7. Add sauce and simmer until thickened. 8. Return chicken and cashews. 9. Cook for 1-2 min or until heated through. 10. Garnish with sliced green onions and chopped cilantro. 11. Serve.

Nutritional info: 450 cal, 30g protein, 35g carbs, 20g fat, 4g fiber.

Orange Chicken

Yields: 4 servings **Prep time:** 20 minutes **Total time:** 40-45 minutes

Equipment: Wok, spatula, thermometer (optional).

Ingredients: 1 lb boneless chicken, 1 egg white, 1 tbsp soy sauce, 1 tbsp rice wine, 1 tsp cornstarch, 1/4 tsp baking soda, pepper, 1/2 cup cornstarch, 1/4 cup flour, 1/4 tsp baking powder, water, 1/4 cup oil, 2 minced garlic, 1 tbsp ginger, orange zest, 1/4 cup green onions, 1/2 cup orange juice, 1/4 cup soy sauce, 2 tbsp vinegar, 2 tbsp sugar, 1 tsp cornstarch, 1/4 cup water.

Instructions: 1. Marinate chicken for at least 30 min. 2. Mix batter ingredients if deep-frying. 3. Stir-fry/deep-fry chicken until cooked. 4. Fry garlic, ginger, and zest in a wok. 5. Add sauce ingredients and simmer until thickened. 6. Return chicken, and add white onions. 7. Cook until heated through. 8. Garnish, serve over rice.

Nutritional info: 450-550 cal, 30g protein, 40-50g carbs, 15-25g fat, 2g fiber.

Honey Garlic Chicken

Yields: 4 servings **Prep time:** 15 minutes **Total time:** 30 minutes **Equipment:** Wok, spatula.

Ingredients: 1 lb boneless chicken, 1 tbsp soy sauce, cornstarch, sesame oil, 2 tbsp oil, 5-6 garlic, 1 tbsp ginger, 1/2 cup broccoli, carrots, 1/4 cup water/broth, 1/4 cup honey, 2 tbsp soy sauce, 1 tbsp vinegar, red pepper flakes, 1 tbsp cornstarch, 1/4 cup water, sesame seeds, green onions.

Instructions: 1. Marinate chicken for at least 15 min. 2. Whisk together the honey, soy sauce, rice vinegar, cornstarch, and water. 3. Stir-fry chicken in hot oil. 4. Remove. 5. Fry garlic and ginger. 6. Add veggies and stir-fry. 7. Add sauce and cook until thickened. 8. Return chicken and add liquid. 9. Cook. 10. Garnish. 11. Serve.

Nutritional info: 400 cal, 25g protein, 35g carbs, 15g fat, 2g fiber.

Lemon Chicken

Yields: 4 servings **Prep time:** 20 minutes **Total time:** 40-45 minutes

Equipment: Wok, spatula, thermometer (optional).

Ingredients: 1 lb boneless chicken, 1 egg white, 1 tbsp soy sauce, rice wine, cornstarch, baking soda, pepper, 1/2 cup cornstarch, 1/4 cup flour, baking powder, water, 1/4 cup oil, 2 minced garlic cloves, 1 tbsp ginger, lemon zest, 1/2 cup broth, 1/4 cup lemon juice, 2 tbsp soy sauce & sugar, 1 tsp cornstarch, 1/4 cup water, lemon slices.

Instructions: 1. Marinate chicken. 2. Mix batter (if deep-frying). 3. Stir-fry/deep-fry chicken until cooked. 4. Fry garlic, ginger, and zest in a wok. 5. Add sauce ingredients and simmer for 2-3 min or until the sauce has thickened. 6. Return chicken. 7. Cook for 1-2 min or until the chicken is heated through. 8. Garnish with lemon slices. 9. Serve.

Nutritional info: 450-550 cal, 30g protein, 40-50g carbs, 15-25g fat, 2g fiber.

Sweet & Sour Chicken

Yields: 4 servings **Prep time:** 20 minutes **Total time:** 40-45 minutes

Equipment: Wok, spatula, thermometer (optional).

Ingredients: 1 lb boneless chicken, 1 egg white, 1 tbsp soy sauce, rice wine, cornstarch, baking soda, pepper, 1/2 cup cornstarch, 1/4 cup flour, baking powder, water, 1/4 cup oil, 1/2 diced onion, 2 bell peppers, 1 can pineapple chunks (juice reserved), 1/2 cup juice, 1/4 cup vinegar, 2 tbsp ketchup & soy sauce, 1 tbsp sugar & cornstarch, 1/4 cup water.

Instructions: 1. Marinate chicken for at least 30 min. 2. Whisk together the 1/2 cup cornstarch, 1/4 cup flour, 1/4 tsp baking powder, and water until you have a thick batter. 3. Cook chicken for 3-4 min per side or until golden brown and cooked through. 4. Fry onion and peppers in a wok for 30 sec or until fragrant. 5. Add juice, vinegar, ketchup, soy sauce, sugar. 6. Thicken with cornstarch slurry. 7. Return chicken, pineapple. 8. Cook for 1-2 min or until heated through. 9. Garnish with lemon slices. 10. Serve over rice.

Nutritional info: 450-550 cal, 30g protein, 40-50g carbs, 15-25g fat, 2g fiber.

Thai Basil Chicken (Pad Krapow Gai)

Yields: 2 servings **Prep time:** 10 minutes **Total time:** 25 minutes **Equipment:** Wok, spatula.

Ingredients: 1 lb boneless chicken, 1 tbsp fish sauce, 1 tsp cornstarch, 1/4 tsp pepper, 2 tbsp oil, 4-6 garlic cloves, 2-4 Thai chilies, 1/2 onion, 1/2 cup green beans, 2 tbsp soy sauce, 1 tbsp fish & oyster sauce, 1 tbsp brown sugar, 1/4 cup water, 2 cups Thai basil, jasmine rice, fried egg (optional).

Instructions: 1. Combine chicken, fish sauce, cornstarch, and pepper. 2. Combine sauce ingredients. 3. Stir-fry chicken in hot oil for 3-4 min or until cooked through and browned. 4. Add garlic and chilies. 5. Stir-fry for 30 sec or until fragrant. 6. Add onion and beans. 7. Stir-fry for 3-4 min or until the veggies are crisp-tender. 8. Add sauce and cook until thickened. 9. Add basil, wilt. 10. Serve over rice and top with egg (opt).

Nutritional info: 450 cal, 30g protein, 40g carbs, 20g fat, 4g fiber.

Pineapple Chicken

Yields: 4 servings **Prep time:** 15 minutes **Total time:** 30-35 minutes **Equipment:** Wok/skillet, spatula.

Ingredients: 1 lb boneless chicken, 1 tbsp soy sauce, cornstarch, sesame oil, 1/4 tsp pepper, 2 tbsp oil, 1/2 diced onion, 2 bell peppers, 1 can pineapple chunks (juice reserved), 1/4 cup juice & soy sauce, 2 tbsp vinegar, 2 tbsp brown sugar/honey, 1 tbsp cornstarch, 1/4 cup water.

Instructions: 1. Marinate chicken for at least 15 min. 2. Whisk together the pineapple juice, soy sauce, rice vinegar, brown sugar or honey, cornstarch, and water. 3. Heat 1 tbsp oil in a wok or large skillet over high heat. 4. Add the marinated chicken and stir-fry or pan-fry for 3-4 min per side or until cooked through and browned. 5. Fry onion and peppers for 2-3 min or until crisp-tender. 6. Add sauce and simmer until thickened. 7. Return chicken, pineapple. 8. Cook for 1-2 min or until heated through. 9. Serve over rice.

Nutritional info: 450-500 cal, 30g protein, 40-50g carbs, 15-20g fat, 2g fiber.

Black Pepper Chicken

Yields: 4 servings **Prep time:** 15 minutes **Total time:** 30 minutes **Equipment:** Wok, spatula.

Ingredients: 1 lb boneless chicken, 1 tbsp soy sauce, 1 tsp cornstarch, 1/2 tsp black pepper, 2 tbsp oil, 3 minced garlic cloves, 1 tbsp ginger, 1/2 sliced onion, 1 sliced red & green bell pepper, 1/4 cup broth, 2 tbsp soy sauce, 1 tbsp oyster sauce, 1 tbsp rice wine, 1 tsp sugar, 1 tsp cornstarch, 1/4 cup water, 1-2 tbsp black pepper, green onions/sesame seeds (optional).

Instructions: 1. Marinate chicken in soy sauce, cornstarch, and pepper for at least 15 min. 2. Heat 1 tbsp oil in a wok over high heat. 3. Add the marinated chicken and stir-fry for 3-4 min or until cooked through and browned. 4. Remove. 5. Stir-fry garlic, ginger, and onion for 30 sec or until fragrant. 6. Add peppers. 7. Cook for 2-3 min or until crisp-tender. 8. Whisk together the soy sauce, oyster sauce, rice wine, sugar, cornstarch, and water. 9. Simmer until thickened. 10. Return chicken and cook for 1-2 min or until heated through. 11. Add 1-2 tbsp of additional black pepper to taste. 12. Garnish and serve.

Nutritional info: 400 cal, 30g protein, 30g carbs, 18g fat, 2g fiber.

Garlic Ginger Chicken

Yields: 4 servings **Prep time:** 15 minutes **Total time:** 30-35 minutes **Equipment:** Wok/skillet, spatula.

Ingredients: 1 lb boneless chicken, 1 tbsp soy sauce, cornstarch, sesame oil, 2 tbsp oil, 4 minced garlic cloves, 1 tbsp ginger, 1/2 onion, 1 bell pepper, 1/2 cup broccoli, 1/4 cup water/broth (opt), 1/4 cup soy sauce, 2 tbsp honey/syrup, 1 tbsp vinegar, red pepper flakes, sesame seeds, green onions (opt).

Instructions: 1. Marinate chicken for at least 15 min. 2. Heat 1 tbsp oil in a wok or skillet over high heat. 3. Add the marinated chicken and stir-fry for 3-4 min per side or until cooked through and browned. 4. Remove. 5. Fry garlic and ginger for 30 sec or until fragrant. 6. Add veggies and stir-fry for 2-3 min or until crisp-tender. 7. (Add water if using a wok). 8. Pour in the chicken broth or water (if using), soy sauce, honey or maple syrup, rice vinegar, and red pepper flakes (if using). 9. Bring to a simmer and cook for 1-2 min or until the sauce has thickened. 10. Return chicken and cook for 1-2 min or until heated through. 11. Garnish and serve.

Nutritional info: 400-450 cal, 30g protein, 20-25g carbs, 15-20g fat, 2g fiber.

Beef Stir-Fries

Mongolian Beef

Yields: 4 servings **Prep time:** 15 minutes **Total time:** 30 minutes **Equipment:** Wok, spatula.

Ingredients: 1 lb flank steak, 1 tbsp soy sauce, cornstarch, 1 tsp rice wine, 1/4 tsp baking soda, 3 tbsp oil, 3 minced garlic cloves, 1 tbsp ginger, 4-5 green onions (cut into 2-inch pieces), 1/4 cup soy sauce, 2 tbsp brown sugar, 1 tbsp hoisin sauce, 1/4 cup water, 1/4 tsp red pepper flakes.

Instructions: 1. Marinate beef in soy sauce, cornstarch, rice wine, and baking soda for at least 15 min. 2. Whisk together the soy sauce, brown sugar, hoisin sauce, water, and red pepper flakes (if using). 3. Heat 1 tbsp oil in a wok over high heat. 4. Add the marinated beef and stir-fry for 3-4 min or until browned and cooked through. 5. Remove. 6. Add garlic, ginger, white onions. 7. Stir-fry for 30 sec or until fragrant. 8. Pour the prepared sauce over the veggies. 9. Bring to a simmer and cook for 1-2 min or until the sauce has thickened. 10. Return beef and add green onions. 11. Cook for 1-2 min or until heated through. 12. Serve over rice/noodles.

Nutritional info: 450 cal, 30g protein, 35g carbs, 20g fat, 2g fiber.

Beef & Broccoli

Yields: 4 servings **Prep time:** 15 minutes **Total time:** 30 minutes **Equipment:** Wok, spatula.

Ingredients: 1 lb flank/sirloin, 2 tbsp soy sauce, 1 tbsp cornstarch, 1 tsp sesame oil, 1/4 tsp black pepper, 2 tbsp oil, 4 minced garlic, 1 tbsp ginger, 2 heads broccoli, 1/4 cup water/broth, 2 tbsp oyster sauce, 1 tbsp soy sauce, 1 tbsp rice wine, 1 tsp sugar, 1/4 tsp red pepper flakes (opt), sesame seeds, green onions.

Instructions: 1. Marinate beef for at least 15 min. 2. Blanch broccoli in boiling salted water for 2-3 min. 3. Heat 2 tbsp oil in a wok over high heat. 4. Add the marinated beef and stir-fry for 2-3 min or until browned and cooked through. 5. Remove. 6. Add garlic and ginger for 30 sec or until fragrant. 7. Add sauces, sugar, flakes (opt). 8. Return beef and broccoli and add water/broth. 9. Cook until sauce thickens. 10. Garnish and serve.

Nutritional info: 350 cal, 25g protein, 20g carbs, 18g fat, 4g fiber.

Pepper Steak

Yields: 4 servings **Prep time:** 15 minutes **Total time:** 30 minutes **Equipment:** Wok, spatula.

Ingredients: 1 lb flank/sirloin, 2 tbsp soy sauce, 1 tbsp cornstarch, 1 tsp sesame oil, 1/2 tsp pepper, 2 tbsp oil, 1 sliced onion, 1 red & green bell pepper, 1/4 cup broth, 2 tbsp soy sauce, 1 tbsp oyster sauce, 1 tsp sugar, 1/2 tsp pepper, 1 tbsp cornstarch, 2 tbsp water, green onions (opt).

Instructions: 1. Marinate beef for at least 15 min. 2. Whisk sauce ingredients (except slurry). 3. Stir-fry beef in 1 tbsp hot oil. 4. Remove. 5. Stir-fry onion and peppers. 6. Add sauce and simmer until the sauce has thickened. 7. Thicken with slurry. 8. Return beef. 9. Cook until heated through. 10. Garnish and serve.

Nutritional info: 400 cal, 30g protein, 25g carbs, 20g fat, 2g fiber.

Orange Beef
Yields: 4 servings **Prep time:** 20 minutes **Total time:** 35-40 minutes

Equipment: Wok, spatula, thermometer (optional).

Ingredients: 1 lb flank/sirloin steak, 1 tbsp soy sauce, cornstarch, sesame oil, 1/4 tsp baking soda, pepper, batter (cornstarch, flour, etc.), 1/4 cup oil, 1/2 sliced onion, 1 orange bell pepper, 2 minced garlic, 1 tbsp ginger, orange zest, green onions, 1/2 cup orange juice, 1/4 cup soy sauce, 2 tbsp vinegar, 2 tbsp sugar, 1 tsp cornstarch, 1/4 cup water.

Instructions: 1. Marinate beef for at least 15 min. 2. Make batter (if deep-frying): whisk together the 1/2 cup cornstarch, 1/4 cup flour, 1/4 tsp baking powder, and water until you have a thick batter. 3. Cook beef. 4. Fry onion and pepper in a wok for 2-3 min or until crisp-tender. 5. Add garlic, ginger, zest. 6. Cook for 30 sec or until fragrant. 7. Add sauce ingredients, simmer, and cook for 2-3 min or until the sauce has thickened. 8. Return beef and green onions. 9. Cook for 1-2 min or until heated through. 10. Serve.

Nutritional info: 450-550 cal, 30g protein, 40-50g carbs, 15-25g fat, 2g fiber.

Ginger Beef
Yields: 4 servings **Prep time:** 15 minutes **Total time:** 30 minutes **Equipment:** Wok, spatula.

Ingredients: 1 lb flank/sirloin, 2 tbsp soy sauce, 1 tbsp cornstarch, 1 tsp sesame oil, 1 tbsp ginger, 2 tbsp oil, 3 garlic cloves, 1 tbsp ginger, 1/2 onion, 1 bell pepper, 1/2 cup broccoli, 1/4 cup broth, 2 tbsp soy sauce, 1 tbsp honey/syrup, 1 tbsp vinegar, 1/2 tsp ginger, 1 tsp cornstarch, 2 tbsp water, sesame seeds, green onions (opt).

Instructions: 1. Marinate beef for at least 15 min. 2. Whisk sauce ingredients (except slurry). 3. Heat 2 tbsp oil in a wok over high heat. 4. Add the marinated beef and stir-fry for 2-3 min or until browned and cooked through. 5. Remove. 6. Fry garlic and ginger for 30 sec or until fragrant. 7. Add veggies and stir-fry for 2-3 min or until crisp-tender. 8. Add sauce and simmer for 1-2 min or until the sauce has thickened. 9. Thicken with slurry. 10. Return beef. 11. Cook for 1-2 min or until heated through. 12. Garnish and serve.

Nutritional info: 450 cal, 30g protein, 35g carbs, 20g fat, 2g fiber.

Black Pepper Beef
Yields: 4 servings **Prep time:** 15 minutes **Total time:** 30 minutes **Equipment:** Wok, spatula.

Ingredients: 1 lb flank/sirloin steak, 2 tbsp soy sauce, 1 tbsp cornstarch, 1 tsp sesame oil, 1/2 tsp black pepper, 1/4 tsp baking soda (opt), 2 tbsp oil, 4 minced garlic cloves, 1 tbsp ginger, 1 sliced onion, 1 red & green bell pepper, 1/4 cup broth, 2 tbsp soy sauce, 1 tbsp oyster sauce, 1 tsp sugar, 2 tbsp black pepper, 1 tbsp cornstarch, 2 tbsp water, green onions (opt).

Instructions: 1. Marinate beef for at least 15 min. 2. Whisk sauce (except slurry). 3. Heat 2 tbsp oil in a wok over high heat. 4. Add the marinated beef and stir-fry until browned and cooked through. 5. Remove. 6. Fry garlic, ginger, onion, and peppers for 2-3 min or until softened and slightly browned. 7. Add sauce and simmer. 8. Thicken with slurry. 9. Return beef. 10. Cook for 1-2 min or until heated through. 11. Garnish and serve.

Nutritional info: 400 cal, 30g protein, 25g carbs, 20g fat, 2g fiber.

Sweet & Sour Beef

Yields: 4 servings **Prep time:** 15 minutes **Total time:** 30-35 minutes

Equipment: Wok, spatula, thermometer (optional).

Ingredients: 1 lb flank/sirloin steak, 1 tbsp soy sauce, cornstarch, 1/4 tsp baking soda, pepper, batter (cornstarch, flour, etc.), 1/4 cup oil, 1/2 onion, 2 bell peppers, 1 can pineapple chunks, 1/2 cup juice, 1/4 cup vinegar, 2 tbsp ketchup & soy sauce, 1 tbsp sugar & cornstarch, 1/4 cup water.

Instructions: 1. Marinate beef for at least 15 min. 2. Make batter (if deep-frying): whisk together the 1/2 cup cornstarch, 1/4 cup flour, 1/4 tsp baking powder, and water until you have a thick batter. 3. Cook beef. 4. Fry onion and peppers for 2-3 min or until crisp-tender. 5. Pour in the pineapple juice, rice vinegar, ketchup, soy sauce, sugar, and cornstarch. 6. Stir to combine. 7. Bring to a simmer and cook for 1-2 min or until the sauce has thickened. 8. Stir in the drained pineapple chunks. 9. Cook for 1-2 min or until heated through. 10. Return beef. 11. Cook for 1-2 min or until heated through. 12. Serve over rice.

Nutritional info: 450-550 cal, 25g protein, 45-55g carbs, 15-25g fat, 2g fiber.

Szechuan Beef

Yields: 4 servings **Prep time:** 15 minutes **Total time:** 30 minutes **Equipment:** Wok, spatula.

Ingredients: 1 lb flank/sirloin, 1 tbsp soy sauce, 1 tbsp rice wine, 1 tsp cornstarch, 1/2 tsp baking soda, 3 tbsp oil, 1 tbsp Sichuan peppercorns, 4-6 dried chilies, 3 garlic, 1 tbsp ginger, 1/2 onion, 1 bell pepper, 1/2 cup broccoli, 1/4 cup broth, 2 tbsp soy sauce, 1 tbsp chili bean/garlic sauce, 1 tsp sugar, 1 tbsp cornstarch, 2 tbsp water.

Instructions: 1. Marinate beef for at least 15 min. 2. Toast & grind peppercorns for 1-2 min or until fragrant and slightly browned. 3. Whisk sauce (except slurry). 4. Heat 1 tbsp oil in a wok over high heat. 5. Add the marinated beef and stir-fry for 2-3 min or until browned and cooked through. 6. Remove. 7. Fry aromatics, chilies, peppercorns. 8. Add veggies, sauce and simmer. 9. Thicken with slurry. 10. Return beef. 11. Cook for 1-2 min or until heated through. 12. Serve over rice/noodles.

Nutritional info: 450 cal, 30g protein, 30g carbs, 22g fat, 2g fiber.

Spicy Korean Beef

Yields: 4 servings **Prep time:** 15 minutes **Total time:** 30 minutes **Equipment:** Wok, spatula.

Ingredients: 1 lb flank/sirloin, 2 tbsp soy sauce, 1 tbsp gochujang, 1 tbsp honey/sugar, 1 tbsp sesame oil, garlic, ginger, pepper, 2 tbsp oil, 1/2 onion, 1 carrot, 1/2 cup mushrooms, green onions, 1 tbsp soy sauce, 1 tbsp gochujang, 1 tsp sesame oil, 1 tsp honey/sugar (all for optional sauce), rice, sesame seeds.

Instructions: 1. Marinate beef in soy sauce, gochujang, honey/sugar, sesame oil, garlic, ginger, and pepper for at least 15 min. 2. Heat 2 tbsp oil in a wok over high heat. 3. Add the marinated beef and stir-fry for 2-3 min or until browned and cooked through. 4. Remove. 5. Stir-fry onion, carrot, and mushrooms. 6. (Opt) Add sauce ingredients and simmer. 7. Return beef and green onions. 8. Serve over rice and garnish with seeds.

Nutritional info: 400 cal, 25g protein, 30g carbs, 20g fat, 2g fiber.

Beef with Snow Peas

Yields: 4 servings **Prep time:** 10 minutes **Total time:** 25 minutes **Equipment:** Wok, spatula.

Ingredients: 1 lb flank/sirloin, 1 tbsp soy sauce, cornstarch, 1 tsp sesame oil, 1/4 tsp baking soda, 2 tbsp oil, 3 minced garlic, 1 tbsp ginger, 1 sliced onion, 8oz snow peas, 1/4 cup broth, 2 tbsp soy sauce, 1 tbsp oyster sauce, 1 tsp sugar, 1/4 tsp flakes (opt), 1 tbsp cornstarch, 2 tbsp water, garnish (opt).

Instructions: 1. Marinate beef for at least 15 min. 2. Whisk sauce (except slurry). 3. Heat 2 tbsp oil in a wok over high heat. 4. Add the marinated beef and stir-fry for 2-3 min or until browned and cooked through. 5. Remove. 6. Fry garlic, ginger, onion for 30 sec or until fragrant. 7. Add peas. 8. Cook for 2-3 min or until the veggies are crisp-tender. 9. Add sauce and simmer. 10. Thicken with slurry. 11. Return beef. 12. Cook for 1-2 min or until heated through. 13. Garnish. 14. Serve.

Nutritional info: 400 cal, 30g protein, 25g carbs, 20g fat, 2g fiber.

Broccoli Beef

Yields: 4 servings **Prep time:** 15 minutes **Total time:** 30 minutes **Equipment:** Wok, spatula.

Ingredients: 1 lb flank/sirloin, 2 tbsp soy sauce, 1 tbsp cornstarch, 1 tsp sesame oil, 1/2 tsp ginger, pepper, 2 tbsp oil, 4 minced garlic cloves, 1 tbsp ginger, 1 head broccoli, 1/4 cup water/broth, 2 tbsp oyster sauce, 1 tbsp soy sauce, 1 tbsp rice wine, 1 tsp sugar, 1/4 tsp red pepper flakes (opt), sesame seeds, green onions (opt).

Instructions: 1. Marinate beef for at least 15 min. 2. Blanch broccoli. 3. Heat oil in a wok. 4. Stir-fry beef until cooked. 5. Remove. 6. Add garlic and ginger. 7. Add sauces, sugar, flakes (opt). 8. Return beef and broccoli and add water/broth. 9. Cook until sauce thickens. 10. Garnish and serve.

Nutritional info: 350 cal, 25g protein, 20g carbs, 18g fat, 4g fiber.

Pork Stir-Fries

Sweet & Sour Pork

Yields: 4 servings **Prep time:** 20 minutes **Total time:** 40-45 minutes

Equipment: Wok, spatula, thermometer (opt).

Ingredients: 1 lb pork, 1 egg white, 1 tbsp soy sauce, rice wine, cornstarch, baking soda, pepper, 1/2 cup cornstarch, 1/4 cup flour, baking powder, water, 1/4 cup oil, 1/2 onion, 2 bell peppers, 1 can pineapple chunks (reserve juice), 2 tbsp garlic, 1 tbsp ginger, 1/2 cup juice, 1/4 cup vinegar, 2 tbsp ketchup & soy sauce, 1/4 cup sugar, 1 tbsp cornstarch, 1/4 cup water.

Instructions: 1. Marinate pork for at least 20 min. 2. Mix batter (if deep-frying). 3. Cook the pork. 4. Fry onion, peppers, garlic, ginger. 5. Add juice, vinegar, ketchup, soy sauce, sugar. 6. Thicken with cornstarch slurry. 7. Return pork and pineapple. 8. Cook for 1-2 min or until heated through. 9. Serve over rice/noodles.

Nutritional info: 450-550 cal, 25g protein, 45-55g carbs, 15-25g fat, 2g fiber.

Kung Pao Pork

Yields: 4 servings **Prep time:** 15 minutes **Total time:** 35 minutes **Equipment:** Wok, spatula.

Ingredients: 1 lb boneless pork, 1 tbsp soy sauce, 1 tbsp rice wine, 1 tsp cornstarch, pepper, 2 tbsp oil, 1 tbsp Sichuan peppercorns, 8-10 dried chilies, 3 minced garlic cloves, 1-inch ginger, 1/2 red & green bell pepper, 1/2 cup peanuts, 3 green onions, 2 tbsp soy sauce, 1 tbsp vinegar, 1 tbsp rice wine, 1 tbsp sugar, 1 tsp cornstarch, 1/4 cup water.

Instructions: 1. Marinate pork for at least 15 min. 2. Toast & grind peppercorns. 3. Whisk together the soy sauce, rice vinegar, honey or maple syrup, cornstarch, and water. 4. Stir-fry pork in 1 tbsp hot oil. 5. Remove. 6. Stir-fry chilies, garlic, ginger for 30 sec or until fragrant. 7. Add peppers. 8. Cook for 2-3 min or until crisp-tender. 9. Return pork; add sauce and peppercorns. 10. Cook for 1 min. 11. Stir in peanuts and onions. 12. Serve over rice/noodles.

Nutritional info: 450 cal, 30g protein, 35g carbs, 20g fat, 4g fiber.

Moo Shu Pork

Yields: 4 servings **Prep time:** 15 minutes **Total time:** 30 minutes **Equipment:** Wok, spatula.

Ingredients: 1 lb pork, 1 tbsp soy sauce, cornstarch, 1/4 tsp baking soda, pepper, 2 tbsp oil, 2 eggs, dried mushrooms (opt), cabbage, carrots, bamboo shoots, green onions, hoisin sauce, 1/4 cup broth, 2 tbsp soy sauce, 1 tbsp oyster sauce, 1 tsp sugar, cornstarch, water.

Instructions: 1. Marinate pork for at least 15 min. 2. Whisk sauce (except slurry). 3. Scramble eggs in 1 tbsp hot oil. 4. Remove. 5. Stir-fry pork in remaining oil for 2-3 min or until browned and cooked through. 6. Remove. 7. Stir-fry veggies and mushrooms for 3-4 min or until the veggies are crisp-tender. 8. Add sauce and simmer. 9. Thicken with slurry. 10. Return pork, eggs, white onions. 11. Cook for 1-2 min or until heated through. 12. Serve with hoisin, pancakes/tortillas, and garnish with sliced green onions (green parts).

Nutritional info: 450 cal, 30g protein, 35g carbs, 20g fat, 4g fiber.

Twice-Cooked Pork (Hui Guo Rou)

Yields: 4 servings **Prep time:** 20 minutes **Total time:** 40 minutes **Equipment:** Wok, spatula, steamer/pot.

Ingredients: 1 lb pork belly, 1 tbsp rice wine, 1/2 tsp salt, ginger, green onions (white parts), water, 2 tbsp oil, 4 sliced garlic cloves, 1 tbsp black beans, 1/2 green & red bell pepper, chilies, green onions (green parts), 2 tbsp soy sauce, 1 tbsp rice wine, 1 tsp sugar, 1/4 tsp pepper.

Instructions: 1. In a large pot, combine the pork belly cubes, rice wine, salt, ginger slices, and green onion white parts. 2. Add the 4 cups of water and bring to a boil. 3. Reduce heat and simmer for 20 min or until the pork is tender. 4. Drain. 5. Stir-fry in hot oil until browned. 6. Remove. 7. Fry garlic, beans, chilies. 8. Add peppers. 9. Add sauce ingredients. 10. Return pork. 11. Toss. 12. Cook for 1-2 min or until heated through. 13. Add green onions. 14. Serve.

Nutritional info: 450 cal, 30g protein, 25g carbs, 25g fat, 2g fiber.

Garlic Honey Pork

Yields: 4 servings **Prep time:** 15 minutes **Total time:** 30 minutes **Equipment:** Wok, spatula.

Ingredients: 1 lb pork, 1 tbsp soy sauce, cornstarch, sesame oil, 2 tbsp oil, 6 minced garlic cloves, 1 tbsp ginger, 1/2 onion, 1 red & green bell pepper, 1/4 cup water/broth (opt), 1/4 cup honey, 2 tbsp soy sauce, 1 tbsp vinegar, red pepper flakes (opt), sesame seeds, green onions (opt).

Instructions: 1. Marinate pork in soy sauce, cornstarch, and sesame oil for at least 15 min. 2. Stir-fry in 1 tbsp hot oil until browned. 3. Remove. 4. Stir-fry garlic and ginger for 30 sec or until fragrant. 5. Add onion and peppers. 6. Cook for 2-3 min or until crisp-tender. 7. (Add water/broth if using wok). 8. Add honey, soy sauce, vinegar, flakes. 9. Bring to a simmer and cook for 1-2 min or until the sauce has thickened. 10. Return pork. 11. Cook for 1-2 min or until heated through. 12. Garnish with sesame seeds and sliced green onions, serve.

Nutritional info: 400 cal, 25g protein, 35g carbs, 15g fat, 2g fiber.

Pineapple Pork

Yields: 4 servings **Prep time:** 15 minutes **Total time:** 30-35 minutes **Equipment:** Wok/skillet, spatula.

Ingredients: 1 lb pork loin, 1 tbsp soy sauce, cornstarch, sesame oil, 1/4 tsp pepper, 2 tbsp oil, 1/2 diced onion, 2 bell peppers, 1 can pineapple chunks (juice reserved), 2 minced garlic cloves, 1 tbsp ginger, 1/4 cup juice & soy sauce, 2 tbsp vinegar, 2 tbsp sweetener, 1 tbsp cornstarch, 1/4 cup water, garnish (optional).

Instructions: 1. Marinate pork for at least 15 min. 2. Whisk together the pineapple juice, soy sauce, rice vinegar, brown sugar or honey, cornstarch, and water. 3. Heat 2 tbsp oil in a wok or large skillet over high heat. 4. Add the marinated pork and stir-fry or pan-fry for 3-4 min per side or until cooked through and browned. 5. Fry onion, peppers, garlic, ginger. 6. Add sauce and simmer. 7. Return pork and pineapple. 8. Cook for 1-2 min or until heated through. 9. Garnish and serve.

Nutritional info: 400-450 cal, 25g protein, 40-50g carbs, 15-20g fat, 2g fiber.

Spicy Korean Pork

Yields: 4 servings **Prep time:** 15 minutes **Total time:** 35 minutes **Equipment:** Wok, spatula.

Ingredients: 1 lb pork, 2 tbsp gochujang, 1 tbsp soy sauce, rice wine/mirin, brown sugar, sesame oil, 1/2 tsp ginger & minced garlic, pepper, 2 tbsp oil, 1 onion, 2 minced garlic, 1/2 green cabbage, 1 julienned carrot, 3-4 green onions, 1 tbsp sesame seeds, red pepper flakes (opt).

Instructions: 1. Marinate pork in all marinade ingredients for at least 15 min. 2. Heat 2 tbsp oil in a wok over high heat. 3. Add the marinated pork and stir-fry for 3-4 min per side or until browned and cooked through. 4. Remove. 5. Add the diced onion, julienned carrot, and shredded green cabbage to the hot wok. 6. Stir-fry for 3-4 min or until the veggies are crisp-tender. 7. Stir in the minced garlic and grated ginger. 8. Cook for 30 sec or until fragrant. 9. Return pork and heat through. 10. Cook for 1-2 min or until heated through. 11. Serve with rice, garnish with sesame seeds and additional red pepper flakes, if desired.

Nutritional info: 450-500 cal, 25g protein, 35g carbs, 20-25g fat, 4g fiber.

Black Pepper Pork

Yields: 4 servings **Prep time:** 15 minutes **Total time:** 30 minutes **Equipment:** Wok, spatula.

Ingredients: 1 lb pork, 1 tbsp soy sauce, cornstarch, 1 tsp rice wine, 1/2 tsp black pepper, 2 tbsp oil, 3 minced garlic, 1 tbsp ginger, 1 onion, 2 bell peppers, 1/4 cup broth, 2 tbsp soy sauce, 1 tbsp oyster sauce, 1 tsp sugar, 2 tbsp black pepper, green onions/sesame seeds (opt).

Instructions: 1. Marinate pork for at least 15 min. 2. Whisk together the soy sauce, oyster sauce, sugar, and black pepper. 3. Heat 2 tbsp oil in a wok over high heat. 4. Add the marinated pork and stir-fry for 2-3 min or until browned and cooked through. 5. Remove. 6. Fry garlic, ginger, onion, and peppers for 2-3 min or until softened and slightly browned. 7. Add sauce and simmer for 1-2 min or until the sauce has thickened. 8. Return pork. 9. Cook for 1-2 min or until heated through. 10. Garnish with sliced green onions and sesame seeds (opt). 11. Serve.

Nutritional info: 400 cal, 30g protein, 20g carbs, 22g fat, 2g fiber.

Green Bean & Pork Stir-fry

Yields: 4 servings **Prep time:** 10 minutes **Total time:** 25 minutes **Equipment:** Wok, spatula.

Ingredients: 1 lb pork loin, 1 tbsp soy sauce, cornstarch, sesame oil, 2 tbsp oil, 3 minced garlic cloves, 1 tbsp ginger, 1 lb green beans, 1/4 cup water/broth (opt), 1/4 cup soy sauce, 1 tbsp oyster sauce, 1 tbsp rice wine, 1 tsp sugar, 1/4 tsp red pepper flakes (opt), sesame seeds, green onions (opt).

Instructions: 1. Marinate pork for at least 15 min. 2. Heat 2 tbsp oil in a wok over high heat. 3. Add the marinated pork and stir-fry for 3-4 min per side or until cooked through and browned. 4. Remove. 5. Stir-fry garlic and ginger for 30 sec or until fragrant. 6. Add green beans, stir-fry. 7. Add water/broth if needed. 8. Add sauce ingredients, simmer. 9. Return pork. 10. Cook for 1-2 min or until heated through. 11. Garnish with sesame seeds and sliced green onions (opt). 12. Serve.

Nutritional info: 350 cal, 25g protein, 20g carbs, 18g fat, 4g fiber.

Ginger Pork with Bok Choy

Yields: 4 servings **Prep time:** 10 minutes **Total time:** 25 minutes **Equipment:** Wok, spatula.

Ingredients: 1 lb pork, 1 tbsp soy sauce, cornstarch, sesame oil, 1 tsp ginger, 2 tbsp oil, 3 minced garlic cloves, 1 tbsp ginger, 2 chopped baby bok choy, 1/4 cup broth/water, 2 tbsp soy sauce, 1 tbsp oyster sauce, 1 tbsp rice wine, 1 tsp sugar, 1/4 tsp red pepper flakes (opt), sesame seeds, green onions (opt).

Instructions: 1. Marinate pork for at least 15 min. 2. Whisk together the soy sauce, oyster sauce, rice wine, sugar, and red pepper flakes (if using). 3. Heat 2 tbsp oil in a wok over high heat. 4. Add the marinated pork and stir-fry for 3-4 min per side or until browned and cooked through. 5. Remove. 6. Fry garlic and ginger for 30 sec or until fragrant. 7. Add bok choy and stir-fry for 2-3 min or until slightly wilted but still crisp. 8. Add water/broth if needed. 9. Add sauce and simmer. 10. Return pork. 11. Cook for 1-2 min or until heated through. 12. Garnish and serve.

Nutritional info: 400 cal, 30g protein, 20g carbs, 20g fat, 4g fiber.

Seafood Stir-Fries

Garlic Butter Shrimp

Yields: 2 servings **Prep time:** 5 minutes **Total time:** 15 minutes **Equipment:** Wok, spatula.

Ingredients: 1 lb shrimp, 1 tbsp cornstarch (opt), 2 tbsp butter, 4 minced garlic, 1 tbsp oil, 1/4 cup white wine (opt), 1/4 cup broth/water, 1/4 tsp flakes (opt), 1 tbsp lemon juice, 2 tbsp parsley, salt, pepper, lemon wedges (opt).

Instructions: 1. Pat shrimp dry and toss with cornstarch (opt). 2. Heat 1 tbsp oil in a wok over medium-high heat. 3. Add the shrimp and cook for 2-3 min per side or until pink and cooked through. 4. Remove. 5. Melt butter and add garlic. 6. Cook for 30 sec or until fragrant. 7. Add wine (opt), simmer. 8. Add broth/water, flakes. 9. Return shrimp. 10. Cook for 1 min or just until heated through. 11. Add lemon juice and parsley. 12. Season with salt and pepper to taste. 13. Serve. 14. Garnish with lemon wedges, if desired.

Nutritional info: 350 cal, 30g protein, 10g carbs, 20g fat, 1g fiber.

Kung Pao Shrimp

Yields: 4 servings **Prep time:** 15 minutes **Total time:** 30 minutes **Equipment:** Wok, spatula.

Ingredients: 1 lb shrimp, marinade (cornstarch, etc.), 2 tbsp oil, peppercorns, chilies, garlic, ginger, peppers, peanuts, green onions, sauce (soy sauce, vinegar, etc.).

Instructions: 1. Marinate shrimp for at least 15 min. 2. Toast & grind peppercorns. 3. Whisk together the soy sauce, rice vinegar, honey or maple syrup, cornstarch, and water. 4. Heat 2 tbsp oil in a wok over high heat. 5. Add the marinated shrimp and stir-fry until cooked through and pink. 6. Remove. 7. Add the minced garlic, grated ginger, dried red chilies, and ground Sichuan peppercorns to the hot wok. 8. Stir-fry for 30 sec or until fragrant. 9. Stir in the sliced red and green bell peppers. 10. Cook for 2-3 min or until crisp-tender. 11. Return shrimp; add sauce and peppercorns. 12. Cook for 1-2 min or until the sauce has thickened. 13. Add peanuts and onions. 14. Cook for an extra 30 sec or until heated through. 15. Serve over rice or noodles.

Nutritional info: 400 cal, 30g protein, 30g carbs, 18g fat, 3g fiber.

Sweet & Sour Shrimp

Yields: 4 servings **Prep time:** 15 minutes **Total time:** 30 minutes **Equipment:** Wok, spatula.

Ingredients: 1 lb shrimp, 1 tbsp cornstarch, 1/2 tsp salt, 1/4 tsp pepper, 2 tbsp oil, 1/2 diced onion, 1 red & green bell pepper, 1 can pineapple chunks (juice reserved), 2 minced garlic, 1 tbsp ginger, 1/2 cup juice, 1/4 cup vinegar, 2 tbsp ketchup & soy sauce, 1/4 cup sugar, 1 tbsp cornstarch, 1/4 cup water, garnish (opt).

Instructions: 1. Coat shrimp and stir-fry in hot oil until cooked through and pink. 2. Remove. 3. Fry onion, peppers, garlic, ginger. 4. Add juice, vinegar, ketchup, soy sauce, sugar. 5. Thicken with cornstarch slurry. 6. Return shrimp and pineapple. 7. Cook for 1 min. 8. Garnish and serve.

Nutritional info: 400 cal, 30g protein, 40g carbs, 15g fat, 2g fiber.

Lemon Garlic Shrimp

Yields: 2 servings **Prep time:** 5 minutes **Total time:** 15 minutes **Equipment:** Wok, spatula.

Ingredients: 1 lb shrimp, 1 tbsp cornstarch (opt), 2 tbsp oil/butter, 4 minced garlic, 1 tbsp zest, 1/4 cup white wine (opt), 1/4 cup broth/water, 1/4 tsp flakes (opt), 1/4 cup lemon juice, 2 tbsp parsley, salt, pepper, lemon wedges.

Instructions: 1. Pat shrimp dry and toss with cornstarch (opt). 2. Fry in hot oil/butter until pink. 3. Remove. 4. Fry garlic and zest for 30 sec or until fragrant. 5. Add wine (opt), simmer. 6. Add broth/water, flakes. 7. Return shrimp. 8. Cook for 1 min or just until heated through. 9. Add juice and parsley. 10. Season with salt and pepper to taste. 11. Serve with lemon wedges for garnish.

Nutritional info: 350 cal, 30g protein, 10g carbs, 20g fat, 1g fiber.

Black Pepper Shrimp

Yields: 4 servings **Prep time:** 10 minutes **Total time:** 20 minutes **Equipment:** Wok, spatula.

Ingredients: 1 lb shrimp, 1/2 tsp salt & pepper, 2 tbsp oil, 4 minced garlic cloves, 1 tbsp ginger, 1/2 sliced onion, 1 sliced red & green bell pepper, 1/4 cup water/broth (opt), 2 tbsp soy sauce, 1 tbsp oyster sauce, 1 tbsp rice wine, 1 tsp sugar, 1 tbsp black pepper, green onions/sesame seeds (opt).

Instructions: 1. Season shrimp: toss the shrimp with the salt and pepper. 2. Stir-fry in hot oil until pink. 3. Remove. 4. Fry garlic and ginger for 30 sec or until fragrant. 5. Add onion and peppers and stir-fry for 2-3 min or until crisp-tender. 6. Add water/broth if needed. 7. Add sauce ingredients, simmer. 8. Return shrimp. 9. Cook for 1-2 min or until heated through. 10. Garnish with sliced green onions and sesame seeds (opt), and serve.

Nutritional info: 350 cal, 30g protein, 15g carbs, 20g fat, 2g fiber.

Shrimp with Lobster Sauce

Yields: 4 servings **Prep time:** 10 minutes **Total time:** 25 minutes **Equipment:** Wok, spatula.

Ingredients: 1 lb shrimp, 1 tbsp cornstarch, salt, pepper, 2 tbsp oil, 2 minced garlic, 1-inch ginger, 2 green onions (separated), 1/4 cup broth, 1/4 cup rice wine, 1 tbsp soy sauce, 1 tbsp oyster sauce, 1 tsp sugar, 1/4 tsp sesame oil, 1 egg, 1 tbsp cornstarch, 2 tbsp water.

Instructions: 1. Coat shrimp in cornstarch, salt, and pepper. 2. Fry in 1 tbsp hot oil until cooked through and pink. 3. Remove. 4. Fry garlic, ginger, white onions. 5. Add broth, wine, soy sauce, oyster sauce, sugar. 6. Drizzle in the egg while stirring. 7. Thicken with slurry. 8. Return shrimp. 9. Cook for 1-2 min or until heated through. 10. Garnish with the remaining green onions (green parts). 11. Serve.

Nutritional info: 350 cal, 30g protein, 20g carbs, 15g fat, 1g fiber.

Spicy Chili Garlic Shrimp

Yields: 4 servings **Prep time:** 10 minutes **Total time:** 25 minutes **Equipment:** Wok, spatula.

Ingredients: 1 lb shrimp, 1 tbsp cornstarch, 1/2 tsp salt, 1/4 tsp pepper, 2 tbsp oil, 6 minced garlic, 1 tbsp chili garlic sauce, 1/2 sliced onion, 1 sliced red & green bell pepper, 1/4 cup green onions, 2 tbsp soy sauce, 1 tbsp oyster sauce, 1 tbsp rice vinegar, 1 tsp sugar, 1/4 cup water/broth.

Instructions: 1. Coat shrimp, fry in hot oil until pink. 2. Remove. 3. Stir-fry garlic and chili garlic sauce for 30 sec or until fragrant. 4. Add onion and peppers and stir-fry for 2-3 min or until crisp-tender. 5. Add soy sauce, oyster sauce, vinegar, sugar, water/broth. 6. Simmer. 7. Return shrimp. 8. Cook for 1-2 min or until heated through. 9. Add onions before serving. 10. Serve over rice/noodles.

Nutritional info: 350 cal, 30g protein, 20g carbs, 18g fat, 2g fiber.

Pineapple Shrimp

Yields: 4 servings **Prep time:** 10 minutes **Total time:** 25 minutes **Equipment:** Wok/skillet, spatula.

Ingredients: 1 lb shrimp, 1 tsp soy sauce & cornstarch (optional marinade), 2 tbsp oil, 1/2 onion, 2 bell peppers, 1 can pineapple chunks (reserve juice), garlic, ginger, 1/4 cup juice & soy sauce, 2 tbsp vinegar, 2 tbsp honey/sugar, cornstarch, water, flakes (opt), garnish (opt).

Instructions: 1. (Opt) Marinate the shrimp in soy sauce and cornstarch for 15 min. 2. Heat 2 tbsp oil in a wok or skillet over high heat. 3. Add the shrimp and stir-fry for 2-3 min or until cooked through and pink. 4. Remove. 5. Add the diced onion, red bell pepper, and green bell pepper to the hot wok. 6. Stir-fry for 2-3 min or until crisp-tender. 7. Stir in the minced garlic and grated ginger. 8. Cook for 30 sec or until fragrant. 9. Pour in the pineapple juice, soy sauce, rice vinegar, brown sugar or honey, cornstarch, and water. 10. Stir to combine. 11. Bring to a simmer and cook for 1-2 min or until the sauce has thickened. 12. Stir in the drained pineapple chunks. 13. Cook for 1-2 min or until heated through. 14. Return the cooked shrimp to the wok and toss to coat with the sauce. 15. Cook for 1-2 min or until heated through. 16. Garnish with sliced green onions and sesame seeds (opt). 17. Serve.

Nutritional info: 400 cal, 25g protein, 35g carbs, 18g fat, 2g fiber.

Shrimp & Snow Peas

Yields: 4 servings **Prep time:** 10 minutes **Total time:** 20 minutes **Equipment:** Wok, spatula.

Ingredients: 1 lb shrimp, 1/2 tsp salt & pepper, 1 tsp cornstarch, 2 tbsp oil, 4 minced garlic, 1 tbsp ginger, 1/2 onion, 8oz snow peas, 1/4 cup broth, 2 tbsp soy sauce, 1 tbsp oyster sauce, 1 tsp sugar, 1/2 tsp sesame oil, red pepper flakes (opt), sesame seeds, green onions (opt).

Instructions: 1. Toss shrimp with cornstarch, salt, and pepper. 2. Heat 2 tbsp oil in a wok over high heat. 3. Add the dredged shrimp and stir-fry for 2-3 min or until cooked through and pink. 4. Remove. 5. Fry garlic and ginger for 30 sec or until fragrant. 6. Add onion and peas and stir-fry for 2-3 min or until the veggies are crisp-tender. 7. Pour in the chicken broth or water, soy sauce, oyster sauce, sugar, sesame oil, and red pepper flakes (if using). 8. Stir to combine. 9. Return shrimp. 10. Cook for 1-2 min or until heated through. 11. Garnish with sliced green onions and sesame seeds (opt). 12. Serve.

Nutritional info: 300 cal, 25g protein, 15g carbs, 15g fat, 2g fiber.

Salt & Pepper Squid

Yields: 4 servings **Prep time:** 10 minutes **Total time:** 20-25 minutes

Equipment: Wok, spatula, thermometer (optional).

Ingredients: 1 lb squid, 1 tbsp cornstarch, 1/2 tsp salt, 1/4 tsp pepper, 2 tbsp oil, 4 sliced garlic, 1-inch ginger (sliced), 2-3 Thai chilies (or flakes), 1/4 cup green onions, 1 tsp sea salt, 1/2 tsp black pepper, 1/2 tsp peppercorns (opt).

Instructions: 1. Toss the squid rings with the cornstarch, salt, and black pepper. 2. Heat 2 tbsp oil in a wok over high heat. 3. Add the dredged squid and stir-fry for 2-3 min or until cooked through and slightly curled. 4. Remove 5. Add the minced garlic, sliced ginger, and Thai red chilies (or red pepper flakes) to the hot wok. 6. Stir-fry for 30 sec or until fragrant. 7. Return the cooked squid to the wok and toss to coat with the aromatics. 8. Cook for 1-2 min or until heated through. 9. Sprinkle with sea salt, black pepper, and Sichuan peppercorns (if using). 10. Toss to combine. 11. Garnish with sliced green onions. 12. Serve.

Nutritional info: 250 cal, 20g protein, 5g carbs, 15g fat, 1g fiber.

Chapter 5: Noodles and Rice

Noodle Dishes

Chicken Lo Mein

Yields: 4 servings **Prep time:** 15 minutes **Total time:** 30 minutes **Equipment:** Wok, spatula.

Ingredients: 1 lb boneless chicken, 1 tbsp soy sauce, cornstarch, sesame oil, 8oz noodles, 2 tbsp oil, 3 garlic cloves, 1 tbsp ginger, 1/2 onion, 1 carrot, 1/2 cup mushrooms, 1/4 cup water/broth, 1/4 cup broth, 2 tbsp soy sauce, 1 tbsp oyster sauce, 1 tsp sugar, 1/4 tsp pepper, 2 green onions.

Instructions: 1. Prep veggies. 2. Whisk together the soy sauce, oyster sauce, sugar, and black pepper. 3. Cook/prep noodles, toss with 1/2 tbsp oil. 4. Stir-fry chicken in 1 tbsp oil. 5. Remove. 6. Fry garlic and ginger until fragrant. 7. Add veggies. 8. Cook until crisp-tender. 9. Add noodles, water/broth (if dried), and sauce and toss. 10. Return chicken. 11. Cook until heated through. 12. Garnish with sliced green onions, serve.

Nutritional info: 450 cal, 25g protein, 50g carbs, 15g fat, 4g fiber.

Shrimp Lo Mein

Yields: 4 servings **Prep time:** 10 minutes **Total time:** 25 minutes **Equipment:** Wok, spatula.

Ingredients: 8 oz lo mein noodles, 1 lb shrimp, 1 tbsp cornstarch, 2 tbsp oil, 3 garlic, 1 tbsp ginger, 1/2 onion, 1 cup mushrooms, 1 cup broccoli, 1/4 cup water/broth, 1/4 cup soy sauce, 1 tbsp oyster sauce, 1 tsp sesame oil & sugar, red pepper flakes (opt), 2 green onions.

Instructions: 1. Cook/prep noodles, and toss with 1/2 tbsp oil. 2. Coat shrimp in cornstarch, salt, pepper. 3. Fry shrimp in 1 tbsp hot oil. 4. Remove. 5. Fry garlic and ginger. 6. Add onion, mushrooms, and broccoli. 7. Stir-fry. 8. Add noodles, water/broth (if needed), and sauce. 9. Toss. 10. Return shrimp. 11. Garnish and serve.

Nutritional info: 450 cal, 30g protein, 50g carbs, 15g fat, 4g fiber.

Beef Lo Mein

Yields: 4 servings **Prep time:** 15 minutes **Total time:** 30 minutes **Equipment:** Wok, spatula.

Ingredients: 1 lb flank/sirloin, 2 tbsp soy sauce, 1 tbsp cornstarch, 1 tsp sesame oil, 1/2 tsp ginger, 8oz noodles, 2 tbsp oil, 3 minced garlic, 1 tbsp ginger, 1/2 onion, 1 cup mushrooms, 1/2 cup broccoli, 1/4 cup water/broth, 1/4 cup broth, 2 tbsp soy sauce, 1 tbsp oyster sauce, 1 tsp sugar, 1/4 tsp pepper, 2 green onions.

Instructions: 1. Prep veggies. 2. Combine sauce ingredients. 3. Cook/prep noodles, toss with 1/2 tbsp oil. 4. Stir-fry beef in 1 tbsp hot oil until cooked. 5. Remove. 6. Fry garlic and ginger. 7. Add onion, mushrooms, broccoli. 8. Add noodles, water/broth (if dried), and sauce. 9. Toss. 10. Return beef. 11. Garnish and serve.

Nutritional info: 480 cal, 28g protein, 52g carbs, 17g fat, 4g fiber.

Singapore Noodles (Xing Zhou Mi Fen)

Yields: 4 servings **Prep time:** 15 minutes **Total time:** 30 minutes **Equipment:** Wok, spatula.

Ingredients: 8 oz rice vermicelli, 1/2 lb shrimp, 4 oz sliced pork, 2 eggs, 2 tbsp oil, 3 minced garlic, 1 tbsp ginger, 1/2 onion, 1 bell pepper, 1/2 cup carrots, 1/4 cup cabbage & bean sprouts, 1 tbsp curry powder, 1/4 cup broth, 2 tbsp soy sauce, 1 tbsp fish sauce, 1 tsp sugar, 1/4 tsp turmeric, red pepper flakes (opt), 2 green onions, lime wedges.

Instructions: 1. Soak noodles. 2. Scramble eggs in 1 tbsp hot oil, remove. 3. Fry shrimp & pork, remove. 4. Fry garlic, ginger, onion, pepper, carrots. 5. Toast curry powder and add the remaining sauce ingredients. 6. Return shrimp, pork, eggs, add cabbage, sprouts, noodles. 7. Toss. 8. Garnish and serve with lime.

Nutritional info: 450 cal, 25g protein, 50g carbs, 15g fat, 3g fiber.

Drunken Noodles (Pad Kee Mao)

Yields: 2 servings **Prep time:** 10 minutes **Total time:** 25 minutes **Equipment:** Wok, spatula.

Ingredients: 8 oz wide rice noodles, 1/2 lb chicken/beef/pork or 8oz tofu, 2 tbsp oil, 3-4 minced garlic cloves, 1-2 Thai chilies, 1/2 onion, 1/2 red bell pepper, 1/2 cup mushrooms, 2 cups Thai basil, 1/4 cup green onions, 2 tbsp soy sauce, 1 tbsp fish sauce, dark soy sauce, oyster sauce, 1 tbsp brown sugar, 1/4 cup water.

Instructions: 1. Soak noodles. 2. Combine sauce ingredients. 3. Stir-fry protein in 1 tbsp hot oil until cooked. 4. Remove. 5. Stir-fry garlic and chilies for 2-3 min or until softened. 6. Add onion, pepper, mushrooms. 7. Add sauce and noodles and toss until softened. 8. Return protein; add basil and onions. 9. Serve hot.

Nutritional info: 500 cal, 25g protein, 65g carbs, 15g fat, 4g fiber.

Pancit Bihon

Yields: 4 servings **Prep time:** 15 minutes **Total time:** 30 minutes **Equipment:** Wok, spatula.

Ingredients: 8 oz rice vermicelli, 1/2 lb chicken, 1/2 lb shrimp, 2 tbsp oil, 2 minced garlic, 1 onion, 1/2 cup carrots, cabbage, 1/4 cup snow peas, 2 green onions (separated), 1/4 cup broth, 2 tbsp soy sauce, 1 tbsp oyster sauce, 1/2 tsp fish sauce, 1 tsp sugar, 1/4 tsp pepper, 1/4 cup water.

Instructions: 1. Soak the rice vermicelli noodles in warm water for 5-10 min or, according to package instructions, until softened. 2. Drain and set aside. 3. Fry chicken in 1 tbsp hot oil until cooked; remove. 4. Fry shrimp in the remaining oil until cooked through and pink. 5. Remove. 6. Fry garlic and onion for 30 sec or until fragrant. 7. Add carrots and cabbage. 8. Cook for 2-3 min or until the veggies are crisp-tender. 9. Add sauce and noodles. 10. Toss. 11. Cook until tender. 12. Return chicken and shrimp. 13. Garnish with sliced green onions. 14. Serve.

Nutritional info: 400 cal, 25g protein, 50g carbs, 10g fat, 3g fiber.

Rice Dishes

Chicken Fried Rice

Yields: 4 servings **Prep time:** 10 minutes **Total time:** 25 minutes **Equipment:** Wok, spatula.

Ingredients: 3 cups cooked rice, 1 tbsp oil, 1 lb boneless chicken, 1/2 tsp salt, 1/4 tsp pepper, 3 minced garlic cloves, 1 tbsp ginger, 1/2 cup chopped onion & carrots, 1/2 cup peas, 2 eggs, 3 green onions (separated), 2 tbsp soy sauce, 1 tsp sesame oil.

Instructions: 1. Prep veggies. 2. Fry chicken in 1 tbsp hot oil, season, remove. 3. Scramble eggs in the remaining oil and remove. 4. Fry garlic, ginger, white onions for 30 sec or until fragrant. 5. Add onion, carrots, peas. 6. Cook for 2-3 min or until the veggies are crisp-tender. 7. Add rice and fry until heated. 8. Return chicken, eggs. 9. Add soy sauce and sesame oil. 10. Cook for 1-2 min or until heated through. 11. Garnish with sliced green onions (green parts). 12. Serve.

Nutritional info: 400 cal, 20g protein, 50g carbs, 12g fat, 2g fiber.

Shrimp Fried Rice

Yields: 4 servings **Prep time:** 10 minutes **Total time:** 25 minutes **Equipment:** Wok, spatula.

Ingredients: 3 cups cooked rice, 1 lb shrimp, 1/4 cup soy sauce, 1 tbsp cornstarch, 2 tbsp oil, 3 minced garlic, 1 tbsp ginger, 1/2 cup onion, 1 cup peas & carrots, 2 eggs, 3 green onions, 1/4 cup soy sauce, 1 tsp sesame oil, salt, pepper.

Instructions: 1. Marinate shrimp for at least 15 min. 2. Fry in 1 tbsp hot oil until cooked. 3. Remove. 4. Scramble eggs in the remaining oil and remove. 5. Fry garlic, ginger, white onions for 30 sec or until fragrant. 6. Add onion, carrots, peas. 7. Cook for 2-3 min or until the veggies are crisp-tender. 8. Add rice and fry until heated through. 9. Return shrimp, eggs. 10. Add soy sauce, sesame oil, salt, pepper. 11. Cook for 1-2 min or until heated through. 12. Garnish with sliced green onions, serve.

Nutritional info: 450 cal, 25g protein, 50g carbs, 15g fat, 2g fiber.

Beef Fried Rice

Yields: 4 servings **Prep time:** 10 minutes **Total time:** 25 minutes **Equipment:** Wok, spatula.

Ingredients: 3 cups cooked rice, 1 tbsp oil, 1/2 lb ground/sliced beef, 1/2 tsp salt, 1/4 tsp pepper, 3 minced garlic, 1 tbsp ginger, 1/2 cup chopped onion & carrots, 1/2 cup peas, 2 eggs, 3 green onions (separated), 2 tbsp soy sauce, 1 tsp sesame oil.

Instructions: 1. Prep veggies. 2. Fry beef in 1/2 tbsp hot oil, season, remove. 3. Scramble eggs in the remaining oil and remove. 4. Fry garlic, ginger, white onions for 30 sec or until fragrant. 5. Add onion, carrots, peas. 6. Cook for 2-3 min or until the veggies are crisp-tender. 7. Add rice and fry. 8. Return beef, eggs. 9. Add soy sauce and sesame oil. 10. Cook for 1-2 min or until heated through. 11. Garnish and serve.

Nutritional info: 450 cal, 20g protein, 50g carbs, 17g fat, 2g fiber.

Vegetable Fried Rice

Yields: 4 servings **Prep time:** 10 minutes **Total time:** 25 minutes **Equipment:** Wok, spatula.

Ingredients: 3 cups cooked rice, 2 tbsp oil, 3 minced garlic, 1 tbsp ginger, 1/2 cup chopped onion, 1 cup broccoli, 1/2 cup carrots & peas, 1/4 cup red pepper, 2 eggs, 3 green onions (separated), 3 tbsp soy sauce, 1 tsp sesame oil, salt, pepper, 1/2 cup tofu/chicken/shrimp (opt).

Instructions: 1. Prep veggies. 2. Scramble eggs in 1 tbsp hot oil. 3. Remove. 4. Fry garlic, ginger, white onions for 30 sec or until fragrant. 5. Add remaining veggies and stir-fry for 3-4 min or until the veggies are crisp-tender. 6. Add rice and fry until heated through. 7. Return eggs, optional protein. 8. Add soy sauce, sesame oil, salt, pepper. 9. Cook for 1-2 min or until heated through and the flavors are combined. 10. Garnish and serve.

Nutritional info (without protein): 300 cal, 8g protein, 45g carbs, 10g fat, 2g fiber.

Egg Fried Rice

Yields: 2 servings **Prep time:** 5 minutes **Total time:** 15 minutes **Equipment:** Wok, spatula.

Ingredients: 2 cups cooked rice, 2 tbsp oil, 2 eggs, 3 garlic cloves, 1/4 cup diced onion, peas & carrots, 2 green onions, 1 tbsp soy sauce, 1/2 tsp sesame oil, salt, pepper.

Instructions: 1. Scramble eggs in 1 tbsp hot oil. 2. Remove. 3. Fry garlic and onion for 30 sec or until fragrant. 4. Add peas & carrots. 5. Cook for 2-3 min or until the veggies are crisp-tender. 6. Add rice and fry until heated through. 7. Return eggs and green onions. 8. Add soy sauce, sesame oil, salt, pepper. 9. Cook for 1-2 min or until heated through and the flavors are combined. 10. Garnish with sliced green onions. 11. Serve hot.

Nutritional info: 350 kcal, 10g protein, 50g carbs, 12g fat, 2g fiber.

Pineapple Fried Rice

Yields: 4 servings **Prep time:** 10 minutes **Total time:** 25 minutes **Equipment:** Wok, spatula.

Ingredients: 3 cups cooked rice, 1 tbsp oil, 1/2 cup diced onion, 1 red bell pepper (diced), 1/2 cup peas & carrots, 1 cup pineapple chunks, 2 eggs, 3 green onions (separated), 2 tbsp soy sauce, 1 tbsp oyster sauce, 1 tsp sesame oil, 1/4 cup cashews/peanuts (opt), salt, pepper, 1/2 cup cooked chicken/shrimp (opt).

Instructions: 1. Prep veggies. 2. Heat 1 tbsp oil in a wok over medium heat. 3. Pour in the beaten eggs and scramble until cooked. 4. Remove. 5. Stir-fry onion and pepper for 2-3 min or until crisp-tender. 6. Add carrots, pineapple. 7. Cook for 2-3 min or until heated through. 8. Add rice and fry until heated through. 9. Return the scrambled eggs to the wok and toss to combine with the rice and veggies. 10. If using, add the cooked chicken or shrimp and stir-fry for 1-2 min or until heated through. 11. Stir in the soy sauce, oyster sauce, sesame oil, salt, and pepper. 12. Cook for 1-2 min or until heated through and the flavors are combined. 13. Garnish with sliced green onions (green parts) and cashews or peanuts (opt). 14. Serve.

Nutritional info (without protein): 350 cal, 8g protein, 50g carbs, 12g fat, 2g fiber.

Yangzhou Fried Rice

Yields: 4 servings **Prep time:** 15 minutes **Total time:** 30 minutes **Equipment:** Wok, spatula.

Ingredients: 3 cups cooked rice, 4 tbsp oil, 1/2 lb chopped shrimp, 4 oz diced char siu pork, 3 eggs, 1/4 cup diced bamboo shoots & carrots, 1/4 cup peas, 2 green onions (separated), 2 minced garlic, 1/2 tsp ginger, 2 tbsp soy sauce, 1/2 tsp sesame oil, salt, white pepper.

Instructions: 1. Chop veggies and onions. 2. Beat eggs. 3. Scramble eggs in 1 tbsp hot oil, remove. 4. Stir-fry shrimp & pork in 1 tbsp oil, remove. 5. Fry garlic and ginger for 30 sec or until fragrant. 6. Add onion, carrots, bamboo shoots, and peas. 7. Cook for 2-3 min or until the veggies are crisp-tender. 8. Add rice and fry until heated through. 9. Season. 10. Return shrimp, pork, eggs. 11. Toss. 12. Cook for 1-2 min or until heated through and the flavors are combined. 13. Garnish with sliced green onions (green parts). 14. Serve.

Nutritional info: 450 cal, 18g protein, 55g carbs, 17g fat, 2g fiber.

Nasi Goreng

Yields: 4 servings **Prep time:** 10 minutes **Total time:** 25 minutes **Equipment:** Wok, spatula.

Ingredients: 3 cups cooked rice, 2 tbsp oil, 2 eggs, 1/2 onion, 2 garlic cloves, 1 tbsp sambal oelek/chilies, 1/2 cup chicken/shrimp (opt), 1/2 cup peas & carrots, 1/4 cup kecap manis, 1 tbsp soy sauce, 1/2 tsp shrimp paste (opt), 1/4 cup green onions, salt, pepper, garnishes (shallots, cucumber, lime).

Instructions: 1. Chop veggies and onions. 2. Scramble eggs in 1 tbsp hot oil. 3. Remove. 4. Fry protein (opt), remove. 5. Fry garlic, onion, and sambal/chilies for 30 sec or until fragrant. 6. Add carrots and peas. 7. Cook for 2-3 min or until the veggies are crisp-tender. 8. Add rice and fry until heated through and slightly crispy. 9. Return the scrambled eggs and cooked protein (if using) to the wok. 10. Toss to combine with the rice and veggies. 11. Add sauces and shrimp paste (opt). 12. Season with salt and pepper to taste. 13. Cook for 1-2 min or until heated through and the flavors are combined. 14. Garnish and serve.

Nutritional info: 400 cal, 15g protein, 50g carbs, 15g fat, 2g fiber.

Ginger Scallion Lobster Rice

Yields: 2 servings **Prep time:** 15 minutes **Total time:** 35 minutes **Equipment:** Wok, spatula, knife/shears.

Ingredients: 1 lobster, 2 cups cooked rice, 3 tbsp oil, ginger (julienned), 4 green onions (separated), 2 minced garlic, 2 tbsp soy sauce, 1 tbsp oyster sauce, 1 tsp rice wine, 1/2 tsp sugar, 1/4 tsp pepper, 1 tbsp cornstarch, 2 tbsp water.

Instructions: 1. Prep lobster. 2. Whisk together the soy sauce, oyster sauce, rice wine, sugar, black pepper, cornstarch, and water. 3. Heat 1 tbsp oil in a wok over high heat. 4. Add the lobster pieces and stir-fry for 2-3 min or until heated through. 5. Remove. 6. Fry ginger and white onions for 30 sec or until fragrant. 7. Add rice and garlic. 8. Fry until heated. 9. Stir to coat and cook for 1-2 min or until the sauce has thickened. 10. Return lobster. 11. Cook for 1-2 min or until heated through. 12. Garnish and serve.

Nutritional info: 550 cal, 40g protein, 50g carbs, 20g fat, 2g fiber.

Chapter 6: Dim Sum and Dumplings

Dim Sum Favorites

Shrimp & Chive Dumplings (Har Gow)

Yields: 24 dumplings **Prep time:** 30 minutes **Total time:** 40 minutes

Equipment: Wok, steamer basket, spatula, bowl.

Ingredients: 1 cup wheat starch, 1/2 cup boiling water, 1 lb raw shrimp, 1/4 cup chopped water chestnuts, bamboo shoots, Chinese chives/green onions, 1 tbsp soy sauce, 1 tsp sesame oil, 1/2 tsp ginger, salt, pepper, 3 tbsp soy sauce, 1 tbsp vinegar, chili oil (opt), onions, sesame seeds (opt).

Instructions: 1. Combine the wheat starch and boiling water in a bowl. 2. Knead until smooth and elastic. 3. Wrap in plastic wrap and let rest for 30 min. 4. Combine the chopped shrimp, water chestnuts, bamboo shoots, Chinese chives or green onions, soy sauce, sesame oil, grated ginger, salt, and pepper. 5. Mix well. 6. Divide dough into 24 and roll thin. 7. Roll each piece into a thin circle, about 3 inches in diameter. 8. Fill, pleat, seal. 9. Boil water in wok. 10. Steam dumplings on parchment in the basket for 10-12 min or until the dumplings float to the surface and are cooked through. 11. Serve with dipping sauce (soy sauce, vinegar, chili oil) and garnish.

Nutritional info (6 dumplings): 200 cal, 12g protein, 25g carbs, 5g fat, 1g fiber.

Pan-Fried Pork Dumplings (Pot Stickers)

Yields: Approximately 30 dumplings (6 servings) **Prep time:** 30 minutes **Total time:** 45 minutes

Equipment: Wok, spatula, small bowl.

Ingredients: 30 wrappers, 1 lb ground pork, 1 cup chopped Napa cabbage, 1/2 cup grated carrot, 3 sliced green onions, 2 minced garlic cloves, 1 tbsp ginger, 2 tbsp soy sauce, 1 tsp sesame oil, 1 tsp sugar, 1/4 tsp pepper, 2 tbsp oil, 1/2 cup water, 1/4 cup soy sauce, 2 tbsp rice vinegar, 1 tsp chili oil (opt), sesame seeds (opt).

Instructions: 1. Combine the ground pork, shredded Napa cabbage, shredded carrots, sliced green onions, minced garlic, grated ginger, soy sauce, sesame oil, sugar, and black pepper. 2. Mix well. 3. Fill wrappers, moisten edges, pleat. 4. Heat 2 tbsp oil in a wok over medium-high heat. 5. Add the dumplings, seam-side down, and cook for 2-3 min or until golden brown and crispy. 6. Pour 1/2 cup water into the wok. 7. Cover and steam for 5-7 min or until the dumplings are cooked through and the water has evaporated. 8. Remove the lid and increase the heat to high. 9. Cook for 1-2 min or until the bottoms are crispy. 10. Serve with dipping sauce (soy sauce, vinegar, chili oil) and garnish.

Nutritional info (6 dumplings): 350 cal, 15g protein, 30g carbs, 18g fat, 2g fiber.

Shrimp Toast (Wok-Fried)
Yields: 8-10 pieces **Prep time:** 15 minutes **Total time:** 25 minutes

Equipment: Wok, spatula, thermometer, slotted spoon.

Ingredients: 8 oz shrimp (minced), 1/4 cup water chestnuts, 1 green onion, 1 tsp ginger, 1/2 tsp sesame oil, 1/4 tsp salt & pepper, 1 beaten egg, breadcrumbs, oil for frying, dipping sauce (opt).

Instructions: 1. Combine the minced shrimp, chopped water chestnuts, chopped green onion, grated ginger, salt, and pepper. 2. Mix well. 3. Spread a thin layer of the shrimp mixture onto slices of bread. 4. Beat the egg in a separate bowl and brush over the shrimp mixture. 5. Coat the bread slices with breadcrumbs. 6. Heat oil to 350°F (175°C). 7. Carefully add the coated bread slices to the hot oil and fry for 2-3 min per side or until golden brown and crispy. 8. Remove the toast from the oil and drain on paper towels. 9. Serve with dipping sauce (opt).

Nutritional info (2 pieces): 300 cal, 15g protein, 25g carbs, 15g fat, 1g fiber.

Dumpling Varieties

Pork & Cabbage Dumplings (Jiaozi)
Yields: 24 dumplings (4-6 servings) **Prep time:** 30 minutes **Total time:** 45 minutes

Equipment: Wok, spatula, steamer basket.

Ingredients: 24 wrappers, 1/2 lb ground pork, 1 cup chopped Napa cabbage, 1/2 cup grated carrot, 3 sliced green onions, 2 minced garlic cloves, 1 tbsp ginger, 2 tbsp soy sauce, 1 tsp sesame oil, 1/2 tsp sugar, 1/4 tsp pepper, 1 tbsp oil, 1/4 cup water, dipping sauce (soy sauce, vinegar, chili oil), sesame seeds.

Instructions: 1. Combine filling ingredients. 2. Fill wrappers, moisten edges, pleat. 3. Steam dumplings in a wok until cooked. 4. Heat oil and pan-fry dumplings until golden. 5. Serve with dipping sauce and garnish.

Nutritional info (6 dumplings): 350 cal, 15g protein, 30g carbs, 18g fat, 2g fiber.

Vegetable Dumplings (Jiaozi)
Yields: Approximately 30 dumplings (6 servings) **Prep time:** 30 minutes **Total time:** 45 minutes (steaming/pan-frying) **Equipment:** Wok, spatula, steamer.

Ingredients: 30 wrappers, 1 cup cabbage, 1/2 cup carrots, mushrooms (shiitake, wood ear), 3 green onions, 2 garlic, 1 tbsp ginger, 1 tbsp soy sauce & sesame oil, 1/2 tsp sugar, 1/4 tsp pepper & salt, 1 tbsp oil, 1/2 cup water, dipping sauce (soy sauce, vinegar, chili oil), seeds.

Instructions: 1. Combine filling ingredients. 2. Fill wrappers, moisten edges, pleat. 3. Steam in a wok until cooked. 4. (Opt) Pan-fry until golden. 5. Serve with sauce, garnish.

Nutritional info (6): 250 cal, 10g protein, 35g carbs, 8g fat, 3g fiber.

Chicken & Mushroom Dumplings (Jiaozi)

Yields: 24 dumplings (4-6 servings) **Prep time:** 30 minutes **Total time:** 45 minutes (steaming/pan-frying)

Equipment: Wok, spatula, steamer.

Ingredients: 24 wrappers, 1/2 lb ground chicken, 1 cup chopped mushrooms (shiitake & white button), 1/2 cup chopped cabbage, 1/4 cup grated carrot, 2 green onions, 2 garlic cloves, 1 tbsp ginger, 2 tbsp soy sauce, 1 tbsp sesame oil, 1/2 tsp sugar, 1/4 tsp pepper & salt, 1 tbsp oil, 1/2 cup water, dipping sauce (soy sauce, vinegar, chili oil), sesame seeds.

Instructions: 1. Combine the ground chicken, sliced shiitake mushrooms, sliced white button mushrooms, shredded Napa cabbage, shredded carrots, sliced green onions, minced garlic, grated ginger, soy sauce, sesame oil, sugar, salt, and pepper. 2. Mix well. 3. Place a spoonful of the filling in the center of each dumpling wrapper. 4. Moisten the edges of the wrapper with water, then fold the wrapper over the filling and pleat the edges together to seal. 5. Bring a large pot of water to a boil. 6. Place a steamer basket lined with parchment paper in the pot. 7. Arrange the dumplings in a single layer in the steamer basket, making sure they don't touch. 8. Cover the pot and steam for 10-12 min or until the dumplings float to the surface and are cooked through. 9. (Opt) Heat 1 tbsp oil in a wok over medium-high heat. 10. Add the steamed dumplings, seam-side down, and cook for 2-3 min or until golden brown and crispy. 11. Serve with sauce and garnish.

Nutritional info (6): 300 cal, 15g protein, 30g carbs, 12g fat, 2g fiber.

Beef Dumplings (Jiaozi)

Yields: Approximately 30 dumplings (6 servings) **Prep time:** 30 minutes

Total time: 45 minutes (steaming/pan-frying) **Equipment:** Wok, spatula, steamer basket.

Ingredients: 30 wrappers, 1 lb ground beef, 1/2 cup chopped Napa cabbage, 1/4 cup grated carrot, 2 green onions, 2 garlic cloves, 1 tbsp ginger, 2 tbsp soy sauce, 1 tbsp sesame oil, 1 tsp sugar, 1/4 tsp pepper & salt, 1 tbsp oil, 1/2 cup water, dipping sauce (soy sauce, vinegar, chili oil), sesame seeds.

Instructions: 1. Combine the ground beef, shredded Napa cabbage, shredded carrots, sliced green onions, minced garlic, grated ginger, soy sauce, sesame oil, sugar, salt, and pepper. 2. Mix well. 3. Place a spoonful of the filling in the center of each dumpling wrapper. 4. Moisten the edges of the wrapper with water, then fold the wrapper over the filling and pleat the edges together to seal. 5. Bring a large pot of water to a boil. 6. Place a steamer basket lined with parchment paper in the pot. 7. Arrange the dumplings in a single layer in the steamer basket, making sure they don't touch. 8. Cover the pot and steam for 10-12 min or until the dumplings float to the surface and are cooked through. 9. (Opt) Heat 1 tbsp oil in a wok over medium-high heat. 10. Add the steamed dumplings, seam-side down, and cook for 2-3 min or until golden brown and crispy. 11. Serve with sauce and garnish.

Nutritional info (6 dumplings): 350 cal, 18g protein, 30g carbs, 18g fat, 2g fiber.

Fried Wontons

Yields: Approximately 24 wontons (4-6 servings as an appetizer) **Prep time:** 20 minutes

Total time: 30 minutes **Equipment:** Wok, spatula, thermometer, slotted spoon.

Ingredients: 24 wrappers, 1/2 lb ground pork, 1/4 cup chopped shrimp & water chestnuts, 2 chopped green onions, 1 minced garlic clove, 1 tsp ginger, 1 tbsp soy sauce, 1 tsp sesame oil, 1/4 tsp salt & pepper, oil for frying, dipping sauce (opt).

Instructions: 1. Combine the ground pork, chopped shrimp, chopped water chestnuts, sliced green onions, minced garlic, grated ginger, soy sauce, sesame oil, salt, and pepper. 2. Mix well. 3. Place a spoonful of the filling in the center of each wonton wrapper. 4. Fold the bottom corner over the filling, then fold in the sides. 5. Roll up the wrapper tightly and seal the top corner. 6. Heat oil in a wok or deep fryer to 350°F (175°C). 7. Carefully add the filled wontons to the hot oil, a few at a time to avoid overcrowding. 8. Fry for 2-3 min or until golden brown and crispy. 9. Remove the wontons from the oil with a slotted spoon and drain on paper towels. 10. Serve the fried wontons hot with your favorite dipping sauce, such as sweet and sour sauce or chili sauce.

Nutritional info (6 wontons): 250 cal, 10g protein, 20g carbs, 15g fat, 1g fiber.

Lamb Dumplings (Jiaozi)

Yields: Approximately 30 dumplings (6 servings) **Prep time:** 30 minutes **Total time:** 45-50 minutes (steaming/pan-frying)

Equipment: Wok, spatula, steamer.

Ingredients: 30 wrappers, 1 lb ground lamb, 1 cup cabbage, 1/4 cup carrot, 3 green onions, 2 garlic cloves, 1 tbsp ginger, 2 tbsp soy sauce, 1 tbsp sesame oil, 1 tsp sugar, 1/2 tsp cumin 1/4 tsp pepper & salt, 1 tbsp oil, 1/2 cup water, dipping sauce (soy sauce, vinegar, chili oil), sesame seeds (opt).

Instructions: 1. Combine the ground lamb, shredded cabbage, shredded carrots, sliced green onions, minced garlic, grated ginger, soy sauce, sesame oil, sugar, ground cumin salt, and pepper. 2. Mix well. 3. Place a spoonful of the filling in the center of each dumpling wrapper. 4. Moisten the edges of the wrapper with water, then fold the wrapper over the filling and pleat the edges together to seal. 5. Bring a large pot of water to a boil. 6. Place a steamer basket lined with parchment paper in the pot. 7. Arrange the dumplings in a single layer in the steamer basket, making sure they don't touch. 8. Cover the pot and steam for 10-12 min or until the dumplings float to the surface and are cooked through. 9. (Opt) Heat 1 tbsp oil in a wok over medium-high heat. 10. Add the steamed dumplings, seam-side down, and cook for 2-3 min or until golden brown and crispy. 11. Serve with sauce and garnish.

Nutritional info (6 dumplings): 380 cal, 20g protein, 30g carbs, 20g fat, 2g fiber.

Chapter 7: One-Pot Meals

Hearty Soups and Stews

Hot & Sour Soup (Suan La Tang)

Yields: 4 servings **Prep time:** 15 minutes **Total time:** 35 minutes **Equipment:** Wok, spatula.

Ingredients: 1/4 cup wood ear mushrooms, 4oz tofu, 4oz mushrooms, 1/2 cup bamboo shoots, 2 green onions (separated), 1 tbsp oil, 2 minced garlic cloves, 1 tbsp ginger, red pepper flakes, 6 cups broth, 1/4 cup soy sauce & rice/black vinegar, 1 tbsp cornstarch, 2 tbsp water, 1 egg, 1/2 tsp white pepper, salt (opt), cilantro.

Instructions: 1. Soak the dried wood ear mushrooms in warm water for 30 min or until softened. 2. Drain and slice. 3. Fry garlic, ginger, and flakes in oil for 30 sec or until fragrant. 4. Add mushrooms and tofu and stir-fry for 3-4 min or until the veggies are softened. 5. Add broth, soy sauce, vinegar. 6. Simmer, season. 7. Thicken with cornstarch slurry. 8. Drizzle in egg. 9. Garnish with onions and cilantro. 10. Serve hot.

Nutritional info: 250 cal, 15g protein, 18g carbs, 13g fat, 2g fiber.

Chicken & Corn Soup (Wok-Style)

Yields: 4 servings **Prep time:** 10 minutes **Total time:** 25 minutes **Equipment:** Wok, spatula.

Ingredients: 1 tbsp oil, 1 lb boneless chicken, salt, pepper, 3 garlic cloves, ginger, 6 cups broth, 1 cup corn, 1/2 cup mushrooms (opt), 1/4 cup carrots, 2 green onions, 1 tbsp soy sauce, 1 tsp sesame oil, cornstarch slurry (1 tbsp cornstarch + 2 tbsp water), 1 egg (opt).

Instructions: 1. Prep ingredients. 2. Fry chicken in oil, season, remove. 3. Fry garlic and ginger. 4. Add veggies and stir-fry. 5. Add broth and simmer. 6. Add soy sauce and sesame oil, and thicken with slurry. 7. (Opt) Drizzle in egg. 8. Return chicken. 9. Garnish and serve.

Nutritional info: 250 cal, 20g protein, 15g carbs, 12g fat, 2g fiber.

Beef & Vegetable Soup (Wok-Style)

Yields: 4-6 servings **Prep time:** 15 minutes **Total time:** 45 minutes **Equipment:** Wok, spatula.

Ingredients: 1 lb beef stew meat, 1 tbsp soy sauce, cornstarch, 1/4 tsp pepper, 2 tbsp oil, 1 diced onion, 2 minced garlic, 1 tbsp ginger, 2 sliced carrots, 1 cup broccoli, 1/2 cup green beans, 1/2 cup cabbage, 6 cups broth, 1 tbsp soy sauce, 1/2 tsp sesame oil, salt, pepper, green onions, cilantro (opt).

Instructions: 1. Marinate beef. 2. Fry in hot oil until browned. 3. Remove. 4. Fry garlic, ginger, onion. 5. Add carrots, broccoli, beans, cabbage. 6. Stir-fry. 7. Add broth, return beef, soy sauce, sesame oil. 8. Season. 9. Simmer until beef is tender. 10. Garnish and serve.

Nutritional info: 350 cal, 25g protein, 20g carbs, 18g fat, 4g fiber.

Seafood Tofu Soup

Yields: 4 servings **Prep time:** 10 minutes **Total time:** 25 minutes **Equipment:** Wok, spatula.

Ingredients: 1/2 lb tofu, cubed, 1/2 lb shrimp, 1/2 cup crab (opt), 1/2 cup scallops, 2 tbsp oil, 2 minced garlic cloves, 1 tbsp ginger, 2 green onions (separated), 1/2 cup mushrooms, 1/2 cup snow peas, 1/4 cup baby corn, 6 cups broth, 1 tbsp soy sauce, 1 tsp sesame oil, salt, pepper, 1 tbsp cornstarch, 2 tbsp water.

Instructions: 1. Prep tofu & veggies. 2. Heat 2 tbsp oil in a wok or large pot over medium heat. 3. Add the minced garlic and grated ginger. 4. Stir-fry for 30 sec or until fragrant. 5. Stir in the shrimp, crabmeat (if using), and scallops. 6. Cook for 2-3 min or until the seafood is cooked through and pink. 7. Add mushrooms, peas, corn. 8. Cook for 2-3 min or until the veggies are crisp-tender. 9. Pour in the vegetable broth, soy sauce, and sesame oil. 10. Season with salt and pepper to taste. 11. Bring to a simmer and cook for 5-7 min or until the flavors have blended. 12. Stir in the cubed tofu and simmer for 2-3 min or until the tofu is heated through. 13. Whisk together the cornstarch and water. 14. Add the cornstarch slurry to the soup and simmer for 1-2 min or until the soup has thickened. 15. Season. 16. Garnish with onions. 17. Serve hot.

Nutritional info: 300 cal, 25g protein, 20g carbs, 12g fat, 2g fiber.

Chinese Cabbage Soup (Wok-Style)

Yields: 4 servings **Prep time:** 10 minutes **Total time:** 30 minutes **Equipment:** Wok, spatula.

Ingredients: 1 tbsp oil, 2 minced garlic, 1 tbsp ginger (opt), 1/2 Napa cabbage (chopped), 1 sliced carrot, 1/2 cup sliced mushrooms, 1/4 cup wood ear mushrooms (opt), 6 cups broth, 1 tbsp soy sauce, 1/2 tsp sesame oil, salt, pepper, 1/4 cup green onions & cilantro (opt).

Instructions: 1. Prep veggies and rehydrate wood ear mushrooms (opt) in warm water for 30 min, then slice. 2. Heat 1 tbsp oil in a wok over medium heat. 3. Add the minced garlic and grated ginger (opt). 4. Stir-fry for 30 sec or until fragrant. 5. Add cabbage, carrots, mushrooms, wood ear (opt). 6. Cook for 3-4 min or until the veggies are softened. 7. Add broth, soy sauce, sesame oil. 8. Bring to a simmer and cook for 5-7 min or until the veggies are tender and the flavors have blended. 9. Season. 10. Simmer until veggies are tender. 11. Garnish and serve hot.

Nutritional info: 150 cal, 5g protein, 15g carbs, 8g fat, 4g fiber.

Tomato Egg Drop Soup

Yields: 4 servings **Prep time:** 5 minutes **Total time:** 15 minutes **Equipment:** Wok, spatula.

Ingredients: 1 tbsp oil, 4 chopped tomatoes, 2 minced garlic, 1 tbsp ginger (opt), 6 cups broth, 2 tbsp soy sauce, 1 tbsp vinegar, 1/2 tsp sesame oil, 1/4 tsp white pepper, salt, 2 eggs, 1 tbsp cornstarch, 2 tbsp water, green onions, cilantro (opt).

Instructions: 1. Fry garlic and ginger (opt) in hot oil. 2. Add tomatoes and stir-fry until softened. 3. Add broth, soy sauce, vinegar, sesame oil, and pepper. 4. Simmer. 5. Thicken with cornstarch slurry. 6. Drizzle in eggs. 7. Season with salt. 8. Garnish with onions and cilantro. 9. Serve hot.

Nutritional info: 150 cal, 8g protein, 12g carbs, 8g fat, 2g fiber.

Spicy Beef Noodle Soup

Yields: 4 servings **Prep time:** 15 minutes **Total time:** 40 minutes **Equipment:** Wok, spatula.

Ingredients: 1 lb thinly sliced beef, 1 tbsp soy sauce, cornstarch, 1 tsp sesame oil, 1/4 tsp baking soda, 2 tbsp oil, 3 garlic cloves, 1 tbsp ginger, 2 chilies (or flakes), 1/2 onion, 4 cups broth, 8oz noodles, 2 tbsp soy sauce, 1 tbsp chili bean/garlic sauce, 1/2 tsp five-spice powder, 1/4 tsp pepper, green onions, cilantro, chili/sesame oil (opt).

Instructions: 1. Marinate beef for at least 15 min. 2. Fry in hot oil until browned. 3. Remove. 4. Fry garlic, ginger, chilies/flakes. 5. Add broth and simmer. 6. Add soy sauce, chili sauce, five-spice, pepper. 7. Simmer. 8. Add noodles and cook. 9. Add beef and onions. 10. Cook until heated. 11. Garnish and serve. 12. Add chili/sesame oil (opt).

Nutritional info: 450 cal, 30g protein, 45g carbs, 18g fat, 2g fiber.

Pork & Vegetable Stew (Wok-Style)

Yields: 4-6 servings **Prep time:** 15 minutes **Total time:** 45 minutes **Equipment:** Wok, spatula.

Ingredients: 1 lb pork shoulder, 1 tbsp soy sauce, cornstarch, 1/4 tsp pepper, 2 tbsp oil, 1 diced onion, 2 minced garlic cloves, 1 tbsp ginger, 2 sliced carrots, 2 cubed potatoes, 1 cup broccoli, 1/2 cup green beans, 4 cups broth, 1 tbsp soy sauce, 1/2 tsp sesame oil, salt, pepper, 1/4 cup sherry/wine (opt), 1/2 tsp five-spice powder (opt), green onions, cilantro (opt).

Instructions: 1. Marinate pork for at least 15 min. 2. Heat 2 tbsp oil in a wok over high heat. 3. Add the marinated pork and stir-fry for 2-3 min or until browned. 4. Remove. 5. Fry garlic, ginger, onion for 30 sec or until fragrant. 6. Add carrots, potatoes, broccoli, beans. 7. Cook for 2-3 min or until the veggies are slightly softened. 8. Deglaze with sherry/wine (opt). 9. Add broth, soy sauce, sesame oil, and five-spice (opt). 10. Season. 11. Simmer until tender. 12. Garnish and serve.

Nutritional info: 400 cal, 30g protein, 30g carbs, 18g fat, 4g fiber.

Chicken & Mushroom Stew (Wok-Style)

Yields: 4 servings **Prep time:** 15 minutes **Total time:** 45 minutes **Equipment:** Wok, spatula.

Ingredients: 1 lb boneless chicken, 1 tbsp soy sauce, cornstarch, 1/4 tsp pepper, 2 tbsp oil, 1 diced onion, 3 minced garlic cloves, 1 tbsp ginger, 8oz sliced mushrooms, 1/2 cup carrots (opt), 1/4 cup snow peas (opt), 4 cups broth, 1/4 cup sherry/wine (opt), 1 tbsp soy sauce, 1/2 tsp sesame oil, salt, pepper, 1 tbsp cornstarch, 2 tbsp water, green onions, cilantro (opt).

Instructions: 1. Marinate chicken for at least 15 min. 2. Heat 2 tbsp oil in a wok over high heat. 3. Add the marinated chicken and stir-fry for 2-3 min or until browned. 4. Remove. 5. Fry garlic, ginger, onion for 30 sec or until fragrant. 6. Add mushrooms and optional veggies. 7. Cook for 2-3 min or until the veggies are softened. 8. Deglaze (opt). 9. Add broth, soy sauce, sesame oil. 10. Season. 11. Simmer until the chicken is cooked. 12. Thicken with slurry. 13. Garnish. 14. Serve.

Nutritional info: 350 cal, 30g protein, 15g carbs, 18g fat, 2g fiber.

Braises and Simmered Dishes

Red Braised Pork Belly (Hong Shao Rou)
Yields: 4-6 servings **Prep time:** 20 minutes **Total time:** 1 hour 50 minutes

Equipment: Wok, spatula, pot/Dutch oven.

Ingredients: 2 lbs pork belly, water, ginger, 1 green onion, 2 tbsp oil, 3 tbsp rock/granulated sugar, 3 garlic cloves, 1-inch ginger, 2-star anise, 2 cinnamon sticks, chilies (opt), 1/2 cup rice wine, 1/4 cup dark soy sauce, 2 cups broth, 1/4 cup light soy sauce (opt), green onions.

Instructions: 1. Place the pork belly in a large pot with the sliced ginger and green onion. 2. Cover with cold water and bring to a boil. 3. Simmer for 5 min, then drain the water and rinse the pork. 4. In a wok or large pot over medium-high heat, add the granulated sugar. 5. Stir constantly until the sugar melts and turns a deep amber color. 6. Carefully add the blanched pork belly to the caramelized sugar and brown on all sides. 7. Add garlic, ginger, spices, chilies. 8. Stir-fry for 30 sec or until fragrant. 9. Add liquids. 10. Simmer covered until tender. 11. Remove the lid and continue to simmer until the sauce has reduced to a thick glaze. 12. Add light soy sauce if needed. 13. Garnish. 14. Serve.

Nutritional info: 550 cal, 35g protein, 20g carbs, 35g fat, 1g fiber.

Lion's Head Meatballs (Shi Zi Tou)
Yields: 4-6 servings **Prep time:** 20 minutes **Total time:** 60 minutes

Equipment: Wok, spatula, steamer (optional).

Ingredients: 1 lb ground pork, 1/4 cup water chestnuts, 2 green onions, 1 tbsp ginger, 1 tbsp soy sauce, 1 tsp sesame oil, salt, pepper, 1 egg, breadcrumbs, 2 tbsp oil, 3 minced garlic, 1 chopped baby bok choy, 1 cup broth, 2 tbsp soy sauce, 1 tbsp rice wine, 1 tsp sugar, green onions.

Instructions: 1. Combine meatball ingredients, form into 4-6. 2. Brown in hot oil. 3. Remove. 4. Fry garlic. 5. Add bok choy. 6. Steam/braise meatballs with sauce ingredients until cooked. 7. Serve with bok choy & sauce over rice/noodles, garnish.

Nutritional info: 450 cal, 30g protein, 35g carbs, 22g fat, 3g fiber.

Braised Fish with Ginger & Scallions
Yields: 4 servings **Prep time:** 10 minutes **Total time:** 30 minutes **Equipment:** Wok, spatula.

Ingredients: 1 1/2 lbs white fish fillets, 1 tbsp soy sauce, 1/2 tsp cornstarch, pinch of white pepper, 2 tbsp oil, ginger (sliced), 3 green onions (separated), 1/4 cup broth, 2 tbsp soy sauce, 1 tbsp rice wine, 1 tsp sugar, 1/4 tsp sesame oil, green onions (chopped), cilantro (opt).

Instructions: 1. Marinate fish. 2. Combine sauce ingredients. 3. Fry ginger and white onions in hot oil. 4. Add fish and cook 2 min/side. 5. Add sauce. 6. Cover and simmer until sauce thickens. 7. Garnish and serve.

Nutritional info: 350 cal, 35g protein, 10g carbs, 18g fat, 1g fiber.

Soy Sauce Chicken

Yields: 4 servings **Prep time:** 15 minutes **Total time:** 60 minutes **Equipment:** Wok, spatula, lid.

Ingredients: 1 whole chicken (cut into pieces), 5-6 ginger slices, 2 green onions (cut), 3 star anise, 1 cinnamon stick, 2 tbsp oil, 1/2 cup dark soy sauce, 1/4 cup light soy sauce, 1/2 cup rice wine/sherry, 1/4 cup sugar/honey, 4 cups water, green onions (chopped).

Instructions: 1. Blanch chicken in boiling water, and drain. 2. Heat 2 tbsp oil in a wok over medium-high heat. 3. Add the sliced ginger and green onions. 4. Stir-fry for 30 sec or until fragrant. 5. Add chicken and brown on all sides. 6. Pour in sauce mixture (soy sauces, rice wine, sweetener, water). 7. Simmer covered until cooked & sauce thickens for 30-45 min or until the chicken is cooked through and the sauce has thickened. 8. Garnish with chopped green onions. 9. Serve hot.

Nutritional info: 450 cal, 40g protein, 15g carbs, 25g fat, 1g fiber.

Braised Tofu with Mushrooms

Yields: 4 servings **Prep time:** 15 minutes **Total time:** 40 minutes **Equipment:** Wok, spatula.

Ingredients: 1 block (14oz) tofu, cubed, 1 tbsp cornstarch, 2 tbsp oil, 1 sliced onion, 8oz sliced mushrooms, 3 minced garlic, 1 tbsp ginger, 1/4 cup water/broth, 1/4 cup soy sauce, 1 tbsp oyster sauce, 1 tbsp rice wine, 1 tsp sugar, 1/4 tsp pepper, 1/2 cup water, chopped green onions, sesame seeds (opt).

Instructions: 1. Coat tofu in cornstarch. 2. Heat 2 tbsp oil in a wok over medium-high heat. 3. Add the tofu cubes and cook for 2-3 min per side or until golden brown and slightly crispy. 4. Remove. 5. Stir-fry onion, mushrooms, garlic, and ginger. 6. Add sauce ingredients & water/broth. 7. Simmer. 8. Return the tofu and add water. 9. Bring the sauce to a simmer and cook for 5-7 min or until the flavors have blended. 10. Add the tofu back to the wok and simmer for 2-3 min more or until the tofu is heated through. 11. If the sauce is too thin, whisk together 1 tbsp cornstarch with 2 tbsp water and add it to the wok to thicken. 12. Garnish and serve.

Nutritional info: 300 cal, 18g protein, 20g carbs, 15g fat, 4g fiber.

Coca-Cola Chicken Wings

Yields: 4 servings **Prep time:** 15 minutes **Total time:** 60-65 minutes **Equipment:** Wok, spatula.

Ingredients: 2 lbs chicken wings, 1 can Coca-Cola, 1 tbsp soy sauce, ginger, garlic (for opt. marinade), 1 tbsp oil, 2 minced garlic, ginger (sliced), green onions, chilies (opt), 1/4 cup ketchup, 2 tbsp soy sauce, 1 tbsp honey, cornstarch (opt), water, green onions (chopped).

Instructions: 1. Marinate wings in Coke & marinade (opt). 2. Heat 2 tbsp oil in a large wok over medium-high heat. 3. Add the marinated chicken wings and stir-fry for 5-7 min per side or until browned and cooked through. 4. Remove. 5. Fry garlic, ginger, green onions, chilies until fragrant. 6. Add Coke, ketchup, soy sauce, and honey. 7. Simmer and cook for 5-7 min or until the sauce has slightly thickened. 8. Return the cooked chicken wings to the wok and toss to coat with the sauce. 9. Cover and simmer until the chicken wings are tender and the sauce has reduced to a thick glaze. 10. Thicken sauce (opt). 11. Garnish and serve.

Nutritional info: 450 cal, 30g protein, 35g carbs, 20g fat, 1g fiber.

Braised Short Ribs

Yields: 4 servings **Prep time:** 20 minutes **Total time:** 2 hours 50 minutes **Equipment:** Wok, spatula.

Ingredients: 3 lbs beef short ribs, salt, pepper, 2 tbsp oil, 3 garlic cloves, ginger, 2 star anise, 1 cinnamon stick, 1 cup broth, 1/2 cup rice wine, 1/4 cup soy sauce, 2 tbsp hoisin sauce, 1 tbsp honey/sugar, red pepper flakes (opt), 2 carrots, 1 onion, bok choy, green onions, sesame seeds (opt).

Instructions: 1. Season ribs with salt and pepper. 2. Sear in hot oil until browned. 3. Remove. 4. Fry aromatics until fragrant. 5. Pour in the rice wine and scrape up any browned bits from the bottom of the pot. 6. Cook for 1-2 min or until the alcohol has evaporated. 7. Add broth, sauces, sweetener, flakes. 8. Return ribs, carrots, onion. 9. Simmer covered until tender. 10. Add bok choy and simmer uncovered. 11. Serve and garnish.

Nutritional info: 650 cal, 45g protein, 20g carbs, 45g fat, 2g fiber.

Chinese Dongpo Pork

Yields: 4-6 servings **Prep time:** 20 minutes **Total time:** 2 hours 50 minutes **Equipment:** Wok, spatula, lid.

Ingredients: 2 lbs pork belly, water, ginger, green onions, rice wine, 1 tbsp oil, 3 tbsp rock/brown sugar, garlic, ginger, star anise, cinnamon stick, 1/2 cup rice wine, 1/4 cup dark soy sauce, 2 cups broth, 1/4 cup light soy sauce (opt), green onions, bok choy (opt).

Instructions: 1. Blanch pork with aromatics & wine. 2. Caramelize sugar in a wok. 3. Sear pork. 4. Add garlic, ginger, spices. 5. Stir-fry for 30 sec or until fragrant. 6. Add liquids. 7. Simmer covered until tender. 8. Reduce sauce and add light soy sauce (opt). 9. Slice, garnish, and serve with rice & bok choy (opt).

Nutritional info: 650 cal, 40g protein, 25g carbs, 45g fat, 1g fiber.

Red-Cooked Beef (Hong Shao Niu Rou)

Yields: 4 servings **Prep time:** 15 minutes **Total time:** 1 hour 45 minutes **Equipment:** Wok, spatula, lid.

Ingredients: 1 1/2 lbs beef chuck/stew meat, 1/4 cup rice wine, 1 tbsp soy sauce, pepper, 2 tbsp oil, ginger (sliced), green onions (separated), star anise, cinnamon, chilies (opt), garlic, 1/2 cup rice wine, 1/4 cup dark soy sauce, 2 cups broth, 1/4 cup light soy sauce (opt), garnish (opt).

Instructions: 1. Marinate beef for at least 30 min. 2. Heat 2 tbsp oil in a wok over high heat. 3. Add the marinated beef and brown on all sides. 4. Remove. 5. Fry aromatics and chilies (opt). 6. Stir-fry for 30 sec or until fragrant. 7. Pour in the rice wine and scrape up any browned bits from the bottom of the pot. 8. Cook for 1-2 min or until the alcohol has evaporated. 9. Add sauces, broth. 10. Return beef. 11. Simmer covered until tender. 12. Reduce sauce. 13. Add light soy sauce (opt). 14. Garnish and serve.

Nutritional info: 450 cal, 40g protein, 15g carbs, 25g fat, 1g fiber.

Braised Eggplant in Garlic Sauce

Yields: 4 servings **Prep time:** 15 minutes **Total time:** 40 minutes **Equipment:** Wok, spatula.

Ingredients: 2 eggplants, cubed, 1/2 tsp salt, 1 tbsp cornstarch, 3 tbsp oil, 6-8 minced garlic cloves, 1 tbsp ginger, 2-3 chilies (opt), 2 green onions (separated), 1/4 cup broth, 2 tbsp soy sauce, 1 tbsp oyster sauce, 1 tbsp rice wine, 1 tsp sugar, 1/4 tsp pepper, 1/2 tsp sesame oil.

Instructions: 1. Toss the cubed eggplant with salt. 2. Let sit for 15-20 min, then rinse and pat dry. 3. Coat with cornstarch. 4. Fry in 2 tbsp hot oil until browned. 5. Remove. 6. Fry garlic, ginger, chilies, and white onions for 30 sec or until fragrant. 7. Add sauce ingredients, simmer. 8. Return the pan-fried eggplant to the wok. 9. Cover and simmer over low heat for 15-20 min or until the eggplant is tender and the sauce has thickened. 10. Garnish and serve.

Nutritional info: 250 cal, 8g protein, 25g carbs, 15g fat, 5g fiber.

Shanghai-Style Braised Pork (Hong Shao Rou)

Yields: 4-6 servings **Prep time:** 20 minutes **Total time:** 2 hours 50 minutes **Equipment:** Wok, spatula, lid.

Ingredients: 2 lbs pork belly, water, ginger, green onions, 2 tbsp oil, 3 tbsp rock/brown sugar, garlic, ginger, star anise, cinnamon stick, 1/2 cup rice wine, 1/4 cup dark soy sauce, 2 cups broth, 1/4 cup light soy sauce (opt), green onions, hard-boiled eggs (opt).

Instructions: 1. Place the pork belly in a wok with the sliced ginger and green onion. 2. Cover with cold water and bring to a boil. 3. Simmer for 5 min, then drain the water and rinse the pork. 4. In a wok over medium-high heat, add the granulated sugar. 5. Stir constantly until the sugar melts and turns a deep amber color. 6. Carefully add the blanched pork belly to the caramelized sugar and brown on all sides. 7. Add the minced garlic, sliced ginger, star anise, and cinnamon stick. 8. Stir-fry for 30 sec or until fragrant. 9. Pour in the rice wine and scrape up any browned bits from the bottom of the pot. 10. Cook for 1-2 min or until the alcohol has evaporated. 11. Pour in the dark soy sauce, chicken broth, and light soy sauce (opt). 12. Bring to a simmer. 13. Cover the pot and simmer over low heat for 2 hours or until the pork is very tender. 14. Remove the lid and continue to simmer until the sauce has reduced to a thick glaze. 15. Remove the star anise and cinnamon sticks. 16. Garnish with sliced green onions and hard-boiled eggs (opt). 17. Serve hot.

Nutritional info: 650 cal, 40g protein, 25g carbs, 45g fat, 1g fiber.

Chapter 8: Sauces and Condiments

Homemade Sauces

Basic Stir-Fry Sauce

Yields: Enough for 4-6 servings **Prep time:** 5 minutes **Total time:** 10 minutes

Equipment: Wok/saucepan, whisk.

Ingredients: 1/4 cup soy sauce/tamari, 2 tbsp oyster sauce, 1 tbsp rice wine/sherry, 1 tbsp honey/sugar, 1 tsp cornstarch, 2 tbsp water, 1 tbsp sesame oil (opt), 1/2 tsp ginger (opt).

Instructions: 1. Whisk together the soy sauce or tamari, oyster sauce, rice wine or sherry, honey or sugar, cornstarch, and water until smooth. 2. Heat the sauce mixture in a wok or saucepan over medium heat. 3. Stir constantly until the sauce has thickened and bubbles around the edges. 4. Remove from heat. 5. Add sesame oil & ginger (opt).

Nutritional info (2 tbsp): 50 cal, 1g protein, 7g carbs, 2g fat, 0g fiber.

Black Pepper Sauce

Yields: Enough for 4-6 servings **Prep time:** 5 minutes **Total time:** 15 minutes **Equipment:** Wok, spatula.

Ingredients: 2 tbsp oil, 2 tbsp peppercorns, 3 garlic cloves, 1 tbsp ginger, 1/4 cup rice wine/sherry, 1/4 cup broth, 2 tbsp soy sauce, 1 tbsp oyster sauce, 1 tsp sugar, 1 tbsp cornstarch, 2 tbsp water.

Instructions: 1. Heat 2 tbsp oil in a wok over medium heat. 2. Add the black peppercorns and stir-fry until fragrant. 3. Add the minced garlic and grated ginger. 4. Stir-fry until fragrant. 5. Pour in the rice wine and scrape up any browned bits from the bottom of the wok. 6. Cook for 1-2 min or until the alcohol has evaporated. 7. Add broth, soy sauce, oyster sauce, sugar. 8. Simmer. 9. Thicken with cornstarch slurry. 10. Serve.

Nutritional info (2 tbsp): 80 cal, 2g protein, 7g carbs, 5g fat, 1g fiber.

Kung Pao Sauce

Yields: Enough sauce for 4-6 servings of stir-fry **Prep time:** 5 minutes **Total time:** 10 minutes

Equipment: Wok, spatula.

Ingredients: 1 tbsp oil, 1 tbsp Sichuan peppercorns, 4-6 dried chilies, 3 minced garlic, 1-inch ginger (minced), 2 tbsp soy sauce, 1 tbsp vinegar, 1 tbsp rice wine/sherry, 1 tbsp honey/sugar, 1 tsp cornstarch, 1/4 cup water.

Instructions: 1. Whisk sauce ingredients. 2. Toast peppercorns in a wok and grind. 3. Heat oil and fry garlic, ginger, and chilies. 4. Add sauce and cook until thickened. 5. Remove and stir in peppercorns.

Nutritional info (2 tbsp): 60 cal, 1g protein, 9g carbs, 3g fat, 0g fiber.

General Tso's Sauce

Yields: Enough sauce for 4-6 servings of stir-fry **Prep time:** 5 minutes **Total time:** 10 minutes

Equipment: Wok, spatula.

Ingredients: 1 tbsp oil, 3 minced garlic, 1 tbsp ginger, 2 chilies (or 1/2 tsp flakes), 1/4 cup broth, 2 tbsp soy sauce, 1 tbsp hoisin sauce, 1 tbsp vinegar, 2 tbsp sugar, 1 tsp cornstarch, 1/4 cup water.

Instructions: 1. Whisk sauce ingredients. 2. Heat 1 tbsp oil in a wok over medium-high heat. 3. Fry garlic, ginger, chilies/flakes. 4. Stir-fry for 30 sec or until fragrant. 5. Pour in the whisked sauce and cook, stirring constantly, until the sauce has thickened and bubbles around the edges. 6. Serve.

Nutritional info (2 tbsp): 60 cal, 1g protein, 10g carbs, 2g fat, 0g fiber.

Orange Sauce

Yields: Enough sauce for 4-6 servings of stir-fry **Prep time:** 5 minutes **Total time:** 10 minutes

Equipment: Wok/saucepan, whisk, small skillet.

Ingredients: 1 tbsp oil, 1 minced garlic clove, 1 tbsp ginger, red pepper flakes (opt), 1/2 cup orange juice, 1/4 cup soy sauce, 2 tbsp rice vinegar, 2 tbsp honey/sugar, 1 tbsp cornstarch, 1/4 cup water, orange zest.

Instructions: 1. Whisk sauce ingredients. 2. Heat 1 tbsp oil in a small skillet over medium heat. 3. Add the minced garlic and grated ginger. 4. Stir-fry for 30 sec or until fragrant. 5. Add the red pepper flakes (opt) and cook for 10-15 sec more. 6. Remove the aromatics from the skillet and set aside. 7. Add the aromatics to the whisked sauce. 8. Stir to combine. 9. Heat the sauce mixture in a wok over medium heat. 10. Stir constantly until the sauce has thickened and bubbles around the edges. 11. Stir in the orange zest. 12. Serve.

Nutritional info (2 tbsp): 50 cal, 0g protein, 12g carbs, 1g fat, 0g fiber.

Teriyaki Sauce

Yields: Enough sauce for 4-6 servings of stir-fry **Prep time:** 5 minutes **Total time:** 10-12 minutes

Equipment: Wok/saucepan, whisk.

Ingredients: 1 tbsp oil, 2 minced garlic, 1 tbsp ginger, 1/2 cup soy sauce/tamari, 1/4 cup mirin, 1/4 cup sake (opt), 2 tbsp honey/sugar, 1 tsp cornstarch, 2 tbsp water.

Instructions: 1. Whisk sauce ingredients. 2. Heat 1 tbsp oil in a wok or saucepan over medium-high heat. 3. Add the minced garlic and grated ginger. 4. Stir-fry for 30 sec or until fragrant. 5. Pour in the whisked sauce and cook, stirring constantly, until the sauce has thickened and bubbles around the edges. This will take about 5-7 min. 6. Serve.

Nutritional info (2 tbsp): 50 cal, 1g protein, 9g carbs, 1g fat, 0g fiber.

Spicy Garlic Sauce

Yields: Enough sauce for 4-6 servings of stir-fry **Prep time:** 5 minutes **Total time:** 10-12 minutes

Equipment: Wok, spatula.

Ingredients: 2 tbsp oil, 6-8 garlic cloves (minced), 1-inch ginger (grated), 1-2 red chilies (opt, chopped), 1/4 cup green onions (white parts only), 1/4 cup soy sauce/tamari, 1/4 cup broth, 1 tbsp rice vinegar, 1 tbsp honey/sugar, 1 tsp cornstarch, 2 tbsp water.

Instructions: 1. Whisk together the soy sauce or tamari, chicken broth, rice vinegar, honey or sugar, cornstarch, and water until smooth. 2. Heat 2 tbsp oil in a wok over medium-high heat. 3. Fry garlic, ginger, chilies (opt), and onions for 30 sec or until fragrant. 4. Pour in the whisked sauce and cook, stirring constantly, until the sauce has thickened and bubbles around the edges. This will take about 5-7 min. 5. Serve.

Nutritional info (2 tbsp): 50 cal, 1g protein, 7g carbs, 3g fat, 0g fiber.

Peanut Sauce

Yields: Enough sauce for 4-6 servings of stir-fry **Prep time:** 5 minutes **Total time:** 10-12 minutes

Equipment: Wok/saucepan, whisk.

Ingredients: 1 tbsp oil, 3 minced garlic, 1 tbsp ginger, 1/4 tsp red pepper flakes (opt), 1/2 cup peanut butter, 1/4 cup soy sauce/tamari, 2 tbsp rice vinegar, 1 tbsp honey/syrup, 1/4 cup coconut milk/water, 1/2 tsp fish sauce (opt), 1 tbsp lime juice (opt), chopped cilantro & peanuts (opt).

Instructions: 1. Whisk sauce ingredients until smooth. 2. Heat 1 tbsp oil in a wok or saucepan over medium-high heat. 3. Fry garlic, ginger, flakes. 4. Pour in the whisked sauce and cook, stirring constantly, until the sauce has thickened and bubbles around the edges. This will take about 5-7 min. 5. Serve with optional garnishes.

Nutritional info (2 tbsp): 110 cal (without oil), 4g protein, 7g carbs, 8g fat, 1g fiber.

Dipping Sauces

Soy Ginger Dipping Sauce

Yields: Approximately 1/2 cup (4-6 servings) **Prep time:** 5 minutes **Total time:** 10 minutes

Equipment: Wok/saucepan.

Ingredients: 1 tbsp oil, 2 tbsp ginger, 1/4 cup soy sauce/tamari, 2 tbsp rice vinegar, 1 tbsp honey/sugar, 1 tsp sesame oil, green onions, red pepper flakes (opt).

Instructions: 1. Heat 1 tbsp oil in a small wok or saucepan over medium heat. 2. Add the grated ginger and stir-fry for 30 sec or until fragrant. 3. Add soy sauce, vinegar, sweetener, sesame oil, & flakes (opt). 4. Simmer, stirring, until thickened. 5. Cool slightly, add onions. 6. Serve as dipping sauce.

Nutritional info (2 tbsp): 50 cal, 1g protein, 6g carbs, 3g fat, 0g fiber.

Chili Garlic Dipping Sauce

Yields: Approximately 1 cup (8-10 servings) **Prep time:** 5 minutes **Total time:** 15 minutes

Equipment: Wok, spatula.

Ingredients: 1/4 cup oil, 6-8 garlic cloves (minced), 2-4 Thai chilies (chopped), 1 tbsp ginger, 1/4 cup soy sauce, 2 tbsp rice vinegar, 1 tbsp sugar, 1/4 tsp fish sauce (opt), 1/4 cup cilantro (opt).

Instructions: 1. Heat 1/4 cup oil in a wok or saucepan over medium-high heat. 2. Fry garlic, ginger, and chilies for 30 sec or until fragrant. 3. Add soy sauce, vinegar, sugar, fish sauce (opt). 4. Bring the sauce to a simmer and cook, stirring constantly, until the sauce has thickened. This will take about 5-7 min. 5. Stir in cilantro (opt). 6. Serve.

Nutritional info (2 tbsp): 50 cal, 1g protein, 4g carbs, 4g fat, 0g fiber.

Sweet Chili Dipping Sauce

Yields: Approximately 1 cup (8-10 servings) **Prep time:** 5 minutes **Total time:** 15 minutes

Equipment: Wok/saucepan, whisk.

Ingredients: 1/4 cup rice vinegar & water, 1/4 cup sugar, 2 tbsp chili garlic sauce/sriracha, 1 tbsp cornstarch, 2 tbsp water, 1 minced garlic clove, 1 chopped chili (opt), salt.

Instructions: 1. Prep garlic, chili (opt), and cornstarch slurry. 2. Whisk together the rice vinegar, water, sugar, chili garlic sauce, cornstarch, and 2 tbsp of water until smooth. 3. Heat the sauce mixture in a wok or saucepan over medium heat. 4. Stir constantly until the sauce has thickened and bubbles around the edges. This will take about 5-7 min. 5. Remove the sauce from the heat. 6. Stir in the minced garlic, chopped chili pepper (opt), and salt to taste. 7. Cool slightly.

Nutritional info (2 tbsp): 40 cal, 0g protein, 10g carbs, 0g fat, 0g fiber.

Peanut Dipping Sauce

Yields: Approximately 1 cup (8-10 servings) **Prep time:** 5 minutes **Total time:** 10-12 minutes

Equipment: Wok/saucepan, whisk.

Ingredients: 1 tbsp oil, 3 minced garlic, 1 tbsp ginger, red pepper flakes (opt), 1/2 cup peanut butter, 1/4 cup soy sauce/tamari, 2 tbsp rice vinegar, 1 tbsp honey/syrup, 1/4 cup coconut milk/water, 1/2 tsp fish sauce (opt), 1 tbsp lime juice (opt), cilantro & peanuts (opt, chopped).

Instructions: 1. Whisk sauce ingredients until smooth. 2. Heat 1 tbsp oil in a wok or saucepan over medium-high heat. 3. Fry garlic and ginger, flakes. 4. Pour in the whisked sauce and cook, stirring constantly, until the sauce has thickened and bubbles around the edges. This will take about 5-7 min. 5. Serve with optional garnishes.

Nutritional info (2 tbsp): 110 cal (without oil), 4g protein, 7g carbs, 8g fat, 1g fiber.

Hoisin Dipping Sauce

Yields: Approximately 1 cup (8-10 servings) **Prep time:** 5 minutes **Total time:** 15 minutes

Equipment: Wok, spatula.

Ingredients: 1 tbsp oil, 3 minced garlic cloves, 1 tbsp ginger, 1/4 cup sliced green onions, 1/2 cup hoisin sauce, 1/4 cup soy sauce, 1/4 cup rice vinegar, 2 tbsp honey/sugar, 1 tsp sesame oil, red pepper flakes (opt).

Instructions: 1. Heat 1 tbsp oil in a wok over medium-high heat. 2. Add the minced garlic, grated ginger, and sliced green onions. 3. Stir-fry for 30 sec or until fragrant. 4. Stir in the hoisin sauce, soy sauce, rice vinegar, honey or sugar, and sesame oil. 5. Bring the sauce to a simmer and cook, stirring constantly, until the sauce has thickened. This will take about 5-7 min. 6. (Opt) Stir in red pepper flakes to taste. 7. Cool slightly, serve.

Nutritional info (2 tbsp): 100 cal, 1g protein, 15g carbs, 4g fat, 1g fiber.

Sesame Dipping Sauce

Yields: Approximately 1/2 cup (4-6 servings) **Prep time:** 5 minutes **Total time:** 10-12 minutes

Equipment: Small saucepan, Whisk.

Ingredients: 1 tbsp vegetable oil, 2 cloves garlic (minced), 1 tbsp grated ginger, 1/4 cup soy sauce (or tamari), 2 tbsp rice vinegar, 1 tbsp toasted sesame oil, 1 tbsp honey or maple syrup (optional).

Instructions: 1. Heat 1 tbsp vegetable oil in a small saucepan over medium heat. 2. Add garlic & ginger and stir-fry until fragrant. 3. Stir-fry for 30 sec or until fragrant. 4. Add soy sauce, vinegar, sesame oil, & sweetener (opt). 5. Bring the sauce to a simmer and cook, stirring constantly, until the sauce has thickened slightly. This will take about 5-7 min. 6. Cool slightly. 7. Serve.

Nutritional info (2 tbsp): 50 cal, 1g protein, 3g carbs, 4g fat, 0g fiber.

Ginger Scallion Dipping Sauce

Yields: Approximately 1/2 cup (4-6 servings) **Prep time:** 5 minutes **Total time:** 10 minutes

Equipment: Wok, spatula, heat-safe bowl.

Ingredients: 1/2 cup oil, 1/3 cup ginger (thinly sliced), 1/2 cup green onions (thinly sliced), 1/4 tsp salt, 1/4 tsp sugar (opt).

Instructions: 1. Slice ginger & onions. 2. Heat 1/2 cup oil in a small wok over medium-high heat. 3. Add the thinly sliced ginger and green onions to the hot oil. 4. Stir-fry for 5-7 min or until the aromatics are fragrant and slightly softened. 5. Transfer the sautéed ginger and scallions to a heat-safe bowl. 6. Add salt & sugar (opt). 7. Pour the hot oil from the wok over the ginger-scallion mixture. Be careful, as the oil will splatter. 8. Cool before serving. 9. Serve.

Nutritional info (2 tbsp): 120 cal, 0g protein, 2g carbs, 13g fat, 0g fiber.

Spicy Mustard Dipping Sauce

Yields: Approximately 1/2 cup (4-6 servings) **Prep time:** 5 minutes **Total time:** 10 minutes

Equipment: Wok/saucepan, whisk.

Ingredients: 1 tbsp oil, 2 minced garlic cloves, 1 tsp ginger (opt), 2 tbsp hot mustard powder, 2 tbsp cold water, 1 tbsp vinegar, 1/4 tsp soy sauce, pinch of sugar.

Instructions: 1. Mince garlic and grate ginger (opt). 2. Heat oil in a wok or saucepan over medium heat. 3. Add minced garlic and grated ginger and stir-fry until fragrant. 4. Whisk mustard powder & water. 5. Add to wok with soy sauce, vinegar, sugar. 6. Cook until the sauce thickens. This will take about 2-3 min. 7. Cool slightly, serve.

Nutritional info (2 tbsp): 40 cal, 1g protein, 3g carbs, 3g fat, 0g fiber.

Sweet & Sour Dipping Sauce

Yields: Approximately 1 cup (8-10 servings) **Prep time:** 5 minutes **Total time:** 10-12 minutes

Equipment: Wok/saucepan, whisk.

Ingredients: 1 tbsp oil, 1 minced garlic clove, 1/4 cup diced onion & green pepper, 1/2 cup pineapple juice, 1/4 cup vinegar, 2 tbsp ketchup, 1 tbsp soy sauce/tamari, 1/4 cup sugar, 1 tbsp cornstarch, 2 tbsp water.

Instructions: 1. Whisk sauce ingredients. 2. Fry garlic, onion, pepper in oil. 3. Add sauce and simmer. 4. Thicken with cornstarch slurry. 5. Serve.

Nutritional info (2 tbsp): 50 cal, 0g protein, 12g carbs, 1g fat, 0g fiber.

Honey Mustard Dipping Sauce

Yields: Approximately 1 cup (8-10 servings) **Prep time:** 5 minutes **Total time:** 10-12 minutes

Equipment: Wok/saucepan, whisk.

Ingredients: 1 tbsp oil, 2 minced garlic cloves, 1 tbsp ginger, 1/4 cup Dijon & whole grain mustard, 1/4 cup honey, 1/4 cup soy sauce/tamari, 2 tbsp rice vinegar, 1/4 tsp pepper, 1/4 cup green onions.

Instructions: 1. Mince garlic, grate ginger, chop onions. 2. Heat oil and fry garlic & ginger until fragrant. 3. Add mustard, honey, soy sauce, vinegar, and pepper. 4. Simmer, stirring, until thickened. 5. Add onions. 6. Cool slightly, serve.

Nutritional info (2 tbsp): 80 cal, 1g protein, 10g carbs, 4g fat, 0g fiber.

Mango Salsa Dipping Sauce

Yields: Approximately 1 cup (8-10 servings) **Prep time:** 10 minutes **Total time:** 15 minutes

Equipment: Wok, spatula.

Ingredients: 1 tbsp oil, 1/2 red bell pepper, 1/2 jalapeño (opt), 1/4 cup red onion, 1 mango, 1/4 cup cilantro, 2 tbsp lime juice, 1/2 tsp salt, pepper.

Instructions: 1. Dice pepper, jalapeño, onion. 2. Dice mango, chop cilantro. 3. Fry pepper, jalapeño, onion in hot oil until softened. 4. Combine with mango, cilantro, lime juice, salt, and pepper. 5. Serve.

Nutritional info (2 tbsp): 40 cal, 1g protein, 9g carbs, 1g fat, 1g fiber.

Chapter 9: Healthy and Light

Vegetarian Delights

Vegetable Lo Mein

Yields: 4 servings **Prep time:** 10 minutes **Total time:** 25 minutes **Equipment:** Wok, spatula.

Ingredients: 8oz dried/12oz fresh lo mein noodles, 2 tbsp oil, 1/2 onion, 2 minced garlic cloves, 1 tbsp ginger, 1 cup broccoli florets, 1 cup sliced carrots, 1/2 cup sliced mushrooms, 1/2 cup snow peas, 1/4 cup soy sauce/tamari, 1 tsp sesame oil & sugar, 1/4 tsp pepper, 1/4 cup water/broth, 2 green onions, sesame seeds (opt).

Instructions: 1. Cook/prep noodles, and toss with 1/2 tbsp oil. 2. Whisk together the soy sauce or tamari, sesame oil, sugar, black pepper, and chicken broth or water. 3. Heat the remaining oil in a wok. 4. Fry garlic and ginger for 30 sec until fragrant. 5. Add onion, carrots, mushrooms. 6. Stir-fry for 2-3 min or until veggies are tender-crisp. 7. Add broccoli and peas. 8. Stir-fry until tender. 9. Add noodles and sauce. 10. Toss. 11. Cook for 1-2 min or until the noodles are heated through and the sauce has thickened. 12. Garnish and serve.

Nutritional info: 350 kcal, 10g protein, 55g carbs, 12g fat, 5g fiber.

Buddha's Delight (Lo Han Jai)

Yields: 4 servings **Prep time:** 20 minutes **Total time:** 35 minutes **Equipment:** Wok, spatula.

Ingredients: 1/4 cup dried wood ear mushrooms, 4-5 dried shiitake mushrooms, 1/2 cup dried lily buds, 1/4 cup dried mung bean noodles, 2 tbsp oil, 1/2 cup chopped onion, 2 minced garlic, 1 tbsp ginger, 1 cup broccoli, 1/2 cup sliced carrots & bamboo shoots, 1/4 cup snow peas, water chestnuts, cashews (opt), 1/4 cup broth/water, 2 tbsp soy sauce, 1 tsp sesame oil, 1/2 tsp sugar, 1/4 tsp pepper.

Instructions: 1. Soak the dried wood ear mushrooms, shiitake mushrooms, and lily buds in warm water for 30 min or until softened. 2. Drain and chop. 3. Prep veggies. 4. Mix sauce ingredients. 5. Stir-fry garlic and ginger in hot oil for 30 sec until fragrant. 6. Add onion, broccoli, carrots, bamboo shoots, peas, and water chestnuts. 7. Stir-fry for 2-3 min or until veggies are crisp-tender. 8. Add rehydrated ingredients & sauce. 9. Pour the prepared sauce over the mixture. 10. Cook for 2-3 min or until the sauce has thickened and the noodles are heated through. 11. Garnish with cashews (opt), serve.

Nutritional info: 300 cal, 10g protein, 40g carbs, 12g fat, 6g fiber.

Vegetable Spring Rolls

Yields: 12 spring rolls (4 servings) **Prep time:** 20 minutes **Total time:** 35 minutes

Equipment: Wok, spatula, thermometer, slotted spoon, bowl with water.

Ingredients: Filling: 1 tbsp oil, 1/2 cup shredded cabbage & carrots, 1/4 cup mushrooms, bean sprouts, 2 garlic cloves, 1 tbsp ginger, salt, pepper. Wrappers: 12 wrappers. Deep Frying: Oil. Dipping Sauce (opt): 1/4 cup soy sauce, 2 tbsp vinegar, 1 tsp sesame oil, chili garlic sauce.

Instructions: 1. Stir-fry filling ingredients in oil. 2. Cool. 3. Place filling on the wrapper, fold & seal with water. 4. Heat oil to 350°F. 5. Fry rolls until golden brown. 6. Serve with sauce (opt).

Nutritional info (3 rolls): 200 cal, 4g protein, 25g carbs, 10g fat, 2g fiber.

Tofu & Vegetable Stir-fry

Yields: 4 servings **Prep time:** 15 minutes **Total time:** 30 minutes **Equipment:** Wok, spatula.

Ingredients: 1 block (14oz) tofu, cubed, 1 tbsp cornstarch, 2 tbsp oil, 3 minced garlic, 1 tbsp ginger, 1/2 cup chopped onion, 1 bell pepper, 1 cup broccoli, 1/2 cup mushrooms, 1/2 cup snow peas, 1/4 cup soy sauce/tamari, 1 tsp sesame oil, 1 tsp sugar, 1/4 cup water/broth, 2 green onions, sesame seeds (opt).

Instructions: 1. Coat tofu in cornstarch. 2. Fry in 1 tbsp hot oil until golden. 3. Remove. 4. Stir-fry garlic, ginger, onion in remaining oil. 5. Add pepper, broccoli, mushrooms, peas. 6. Stir-fry for 3-5 min or until the veggies are crisp-tender. 7. Add sauce ingredients. 8. Return the tofu to the wok and toss to coat with the sauce. 9. Cook for 1-2 min or until the tofu is heated through. 10. Garnish with sliced green onions and sesame seeds (opt). 11. Serve.

Nutritional info: 350 cal, 18g protein, 30g carbs, 18g fat, 5g fiber.

Low-Calorie Options

Steamed Fish with Ginger and Scallions

Yields: 4 servings **Prep time:** 10 minutes **Total time:** 25 minutes **Equipment:** Wok, steamer basket, spatula.

Ingredients: 1 whole fish, 1 tbsp rice wine, 1/2 tsp salt, ginger (sliced/julienned), green onions, 2 tbsp soy sauce, 1 tbsp sesame oil.

Instructions: 1. Make several shallow slits on both sides of the fish to allow the sauce to penetrate. 2. Season the fish inside and out with rice wine and salt. 3. Boil water in wok. 4. Place fish on a plate and add half of ginger & onions. 5. Cover the pot and steam for 15-20 min or until the fish is cooked through and flakes easily with a fork. 6. The fish will be ready when it turns opaque, and the skin is easily peeled off. 7. Mix soy sauce & oil. 8. Remove fish and discard old aromatics. 9. Drizzle sauce and garnish with fresh ginger & onions. 10. Serve hot with rice.

Nutritional info: 300 cal, 35g protein, 5g carbs, 15g fat, 1g fiber.

Shrimp and Broccoli Stir-fry

Yields: 4 servings **Prep time:** 10 minutes **Total time:** 25 minutes **Equipment:** Wok, spatula.

Ingredients: 1 lb shrimp, 1 tbsp cornstarch, 1/2 tsp salt, 1/4 tsp pepper, 2 tbsp oil, 4 minced garlic, 1 tbsp ginger, 2 cups broccoli, 1/2 red bell pepper, 1/4 cup broth, 2 tbsp soy sauce/tamari, 1 tbsp oyster sauce, 1 tsp sugar, 1/4 tsp flakes (opt), garnish (opt).

Instructions: 1. Combine the shrimp, cornstarch, salt, and pepper. 2. Toss to coat and marinate for 10-15 min. 3. Bring a large pot of salted water to a boil. 4. Add the broccoli florets and blanch for 2-3 min or until bright green and slightly tender. 5. Drain and set aside. 6. Fry shrimp in 1 tbsp hot oil. 7. Remove. 8. Fry garlic and ginger. 9. Add pepper and stir-fry. 10. Add sauce ingredients, simmer. 11. Return shrimp and broccoli. 12. Cook for 1-2 min or until the shrimp is heated through and the sauce has thickened. 13. Garnish. 14. Serve.

Nutritional info: 350 cal, 30g protein, 20g carbs, 18g fat, 4g fiber.

Chicken Lettuce Wraps

Yields: 4 servings **Prep time:** 10 minutes **Total time:** 25 minutes **Equipment:** Wok, spatula.

Ingredients: 1 lb ground chicken, 1 tbsp soy sauce, 1/2 tsp sesame oil, 1/4 tsp pepper, 2 tbsp oil, 4 minced garlic cloves, 1 tbsp ginger, 1/2 diced onion, 1 diced red bell pepper, 8oz diced water chestnuts, 1/4 cup chopped green onions, 3 tbsp hoisin sauce, 2 tbsp soy sauce, 1 tbsp rice vinegar, 1 tsp sesame oil, 1 head butter lettuce.

Instructions: 1. Prep veggies & onions. 2. Combine sauce ingredients. 3. Stir-fry chicken in hot oil until cooked. 4. Add garlic, ginger, onion. 5. Stir-fry for 30 sec or until fragrant. 6. Add pepper and water chestnuts. 7. Cook for 3-5 min or until the veggies are crisp-tender. 8. Pour in the whisked sauce and cook, stirring constantly, until the sauce has thickened. 9. Spoon the cooked chicken and vegetable mixture into the butter lettuce leaves. 10. Top with chopped green onions. 11. Serve.

Nutritional info (2 wraps): 350 cal, 25g protein, 20g carbs, 18g fat, 2g fiber.

Tofu and Vegetable Soup

Yields: 4 servings **Prep time:** 15 minutes **Total time:** 35 minutes **Equipment:** Wok, spatula.

Ingredients: 1 block (14 oz) tofu, 1 tbsp cornstarch, 1/4 tsp salt & pepper, 2 tbsp oil, 3 minced garlic, 1 tbsp ginger, 1 diced onion, 1 cup broccoli, 1 cup carrots, 1/2 cup mushrooms, 6 cups broth, 1 tbsp soy sauce/tamari, 1 tsp sesame oil, salt, pepper, chopped green onions & cilantro.

Instructions: 1. Toss the cubed tofu with the cornstarch, salt, and pepper. 2. Heat 1 tbsp oil in a wok over medium-high heat. 3. Add the tofu cubes and cook for 2-3 min per side or until golden brown and slightly crispy. 4. Remove. 5. Fry garlic, ginger, onion in remaining oil. 6. Add veggies and stir-fry. 7. Add broth, soy sauce, sesame oil. 8. Season. 9. Return tofu and simmer until heated. 10. Garnish and serve.

Nutritional info: 250 cal, 15g protein, 20g carbs, 12g fat, 4g fiber.

Clear Broth Noodle Soup

Yields: 4 servings **Prep time:** 10 minutes **Total time:** 25 minutes **Equipment:** Wok, spatula.

Ingredients: 8oz noodles, 1 tbsp oil, 2 minced garlic, ginger (sliced), 2 green onions (separated), 1/2 cup mushrooms, 1/2 cup bok choy, 6 cups broth, 2 tbsp soy sauce, 1 tsp sesame oil, 1/4 tsp pepper, salt, 1/2 lb cooked chicken/beef (opt), chopped green onions & cilantro.

Instructions: 1. Cook/prep noodles. 2. Fry garlic and ginger in oil for 30 sec or until fragrant. 3. Add mushrooms and bok choy. 4. Cook for 2-3 min or until the veggies are softened. 5. Add broth, soy sauce, sesame oil, and pepper. 6. Simmer. 7. Season. 8. Add noodles and protein (opt). 9. Cook until heated. 10. Garnish and serve.

Nutritional info (without protein): 200 cal, 8g protein, 25g carbs, 7g fat, 2g fiber.

Steamed Dumplings (Jiaozi)

Yields: Approximately 30 dumplings (6 servings) **Prep time:** 30 minutes **Total time:** 40-42 minutes

Equipment: Wok, steamer, spatula.

Ingredients: 30 wrappers, Filling (choose one or mix): Pork & Chive: 1/2 lb ground pork, 1 cup chives/onions, ginger, garlic, soy sauce, sesame oil, sugar, pepper, salt. Shrimp & Pork: 1/2 lb ground pork & shrimp, carrot, green onions, garlic, ginger, soy sauce, sesame oil, sugar, pepper. Water, cabbage leaves (opt), dipping sauce (soy sauce, vinegar, chili oil), sesame seeds (opt).

Instructions: 1. Combine filling ingredients. 2. Place filling on the wrapper, moisten edges, and pleat to seal. 3. Bring a large pot of water to a boil. 4. Place a steamer basket lined with parchment paper in the pot. 5. Arrange the dumplings in a single layer in the steamer basket, making sure they don't touch. 6. Cover the pot and steam for 10-12 min or until the dumplings float to the surface and are cooked through. 7. Serve with sauce and garnish.

Nutritional info (6 dumplings): 280-330 cal, 12-15g protein, 25-30g carbs, 15-20g fat, 1-2g fiber.

Stir-fried Cabbage with Garlic

Yields: 4 servings **Prep time:** 5 minutes **Total time:** 15 minutes **Equipment:** Wok, spatula.

Ingredients: 1 head cabbage, 2 tbsp oil, 6-8 garlic cloves, 1 tsp ginger (opt), 1 tbsp soy sauce/tamari, 1 tbsp oyster sauce, 1/2 tsp sesame oil, 1/4 tsp red pepper flakes (opt), salt, 1/4 cup water/broth (opt), green onions (opt).

Instructions: 1. Slice cabbage, mince garlic, grate ginger (opt). 2. Heat 2 tbsp oil in a wok over medium-high heat. 3. Add the minced garlic and grated ginger. 4. Stir-fry for 30 sec or until fragrant. 5. Add cabbage and stir-fry until slightly wilted. 6. Add sauces, flakes, and salt. 7. Cook until tender-crisp; add water/broth if needed. 8. Garnish and serve.

Nutritional info: 100 cal, 2g protein, 8g carbs, 7g fat, 2g fiber.

Chicken and Mushroom Stir-fry (light on the sauce)

Yields: 4 servings **Prep time:** 15 minutes **Total time:** 30 minutes **Equipment:** Wok, spatula.

Ingredients: 1 lb boneless chicken, 1 tbsp soy sauce, 1 tsp cornstarch, 1/4 tsp pepper, 2 tbsp oil, 8 oz mushrooms, 3 minced garlic, 1 tbsp ginger, 1/2 onion, 1 bell pepper (opt), 1/4 cup water/broth, 1 tbsp soy sauce, 1 tbsp oyster sauce, 1 tsp sesame oil, 1/4 tsp sugar, green onions, sesame seeds (opt).

Instructions: 1. Marinate chicken for at least 15 min. 2. Stir-fry in 1 tbsp hot oil until cooked. 3. Remove. 4. Stir-fry mushrooms. 5. Cook for 2-3 min or until softened. 6. Add garlic, ginger, onion. 7. Cook for 30 sec or until fragrant. 8. Add pepper (opt). 9. Cook for 2-3 min more or until the veggies are softened. 10. Add sauce ingredients & liquid. 11. Simmer. 12. Return chicken. 13. Cook for 1-2 min or until the chicken is heated through and the sauce has thickened slightly. 14. Garnish and serve.

Nutritional info: 350 cal, 30g protein, 15g carbs, 18g fat, 2g fiber.

Spicy Tofu Lettuce Wraps

Yields: 4 servings **Prep time:** 15 minutes **Total time:** 30 minutes **Equipment:** Wok, spatula.

Ingredients: 1 block (14oz) tofu, crumbled, 1 tbsp cornstarch, 2 tbsp oil, 3 minced garlic, 1 tbsp ginger, 1/2 diced onion, 1 diced red bell pepper, 1 minced jalapeno (opt), 1/4 cup water chestnuts (opt), 1/4 cup soy sauce/tamari, 2 tbsp hoisin sauce, 1 tbsp chili garlic sauce/sriracha, 1 tbsp vinegar, 1 tsp sesame oil, 1/4 cup water, lettuce leaves, green onions, cilantro, peanuts (opt).

Instructions: 1. Coat tofu in cornstarch. 2. Fry in 1 tbsp hot oil until golden. 3. Remove. 4. Stir-fry garlic, ginger, onion, pepper, and jalapeno (opt) in the remaining oil. 5. Add water chestnuts (opt). 6. Add sauce ingredients, simmer. 7. Return tofu. 8. Toss. 9. Cook for 1-2 min or until the tofu is heated through and the sauce has thickened. 10. Serve in lettuce leaves, garnish.

Nutritional info (2 wraps): 350 cal, 18g protein, 25g carbs, 20g fat, 4g fiber.

Cold Sesame Noodles (with Wok-Toasted Sesame Oil)

Yields: 4 servings **Prep time:** 10 minutes **Total time:** 20 minutes **Equipment:** Wok, spatula.

Ingredients: 8 oz noodles, 3 tbsp sesame oil, 1/4 cup soy sauce/tamari, 2 tbsp vinegar, 2 tbsp honey/agave, 1 tbsp sesame paste, 1 tsp chili oil, garlic, ginger, 1/4 cup cucumber, green onions, sesame seeds.

Instructions: 1. Cook noodles, drain, rinse, toss with 1 tbsp sesame oil. 2. Heat the remaining 2 tbsp sesame oil in a wok over medium-high heat. 3. Cook until the oil starts to smoke and turns a darker color. This will take 1-2 min. 4. Remove from heat and let cool slightly. 5. Whisk warm oil with sauces, paste, chili oil, garlic, ginger. 6. Toss with noodles. 7. Garnish with cucumber, onions, and seeds. 8. Serve.

Nutritional info: 400 cal, 10g protein, 55g carbs, 18g fat, 2g fiber.

Chapter 10: International Wok Recipes

Chinese Cuisine

Kung Pao Chicken (Wok-Style)

Yields: 4 servings **Prep time:** 15 minutes **Total time:** 35 minutes **Equipment:** Wok, spatula.

Ingredients: 1 lb boneless chicken, 1 tbsp cornstarch, 1 tbsp soy sauce, 1/2 tbsp Shaoxing wine/dry sherry, 1/4 tsp white pepper, 2 tbsp oil, 1 tbsp Sichuan peppercorns, 8-10 dried red chilies, 3 minced garlic cloves, 1-inch minced ginger, 1/2 red & 1/2 green bell pepper (diced), 1/2 cup peanuts, 3 green onions (sliced), 2 tbsp soy sauce, 1 tbsp Chinkiang/black vinegar, 1 tbsp Shaoxing wine/dry sherry, 1 tbsp sugar, 1 tsp cornstarch, 1/4 cup water.

Instructions: 1. Marinate chicken in cornstarch, soy sauce, wine/sherry, and pepper for 10 mins. 2. Toast peppercorns, grind. 3. Mix sauce ingredients. 4. Stir-fry chicken in 1 tbsp hot oil until cooked. 5. Remove. 6. Stir-fry chilies, garlic, ginger. 7. Add peppers and stir-fry until crisp-tender. 8. Return chicken, add sauce and peppercorns. 9. Cook for 1 min. 10. Add peanuts and onions. 11. Serve over rice.

Nutritional info (approx per serving): 550 cal, 30g protein, 25g carbs, 35g fat, 5g fiber.

Mapo Tofu

Yields: 4 servings **Prep time:** 10 minutes **Total time:** 25 minutes **Equipment:** Wok, spatula.

Ingredients: 1 block (14 oz) tofu, 1 tbsp cornstarch (opt), 2 tbsp oil, 1/4 cup doubanjiang/chili garlic sauce, 1 tbsp black beans, 3 minced garlic, 1 tbsp ginger, green onions (separated), 1/4 cup water/broth, 2 tbsp soy sauce, 1 tsp sugar, 1/4 tsp peppercorns (opt), green onions, sesame oil (opt).

Instructions: 1. Press the tofu between paper towels for 15-20 min to remove excess moisture. 2. Cut tofu into cubes. 3. (Opt) Toss tofu with cornstarch to help it absorb the sauce. 4. Heat oil in a wok over medium-high heat. 5. Add doubanjiang, black bean paste, garlic, and ginger. 6. Stir-fry for 30 sec or until fragrant. 7. Add water or broth and bring to a simmer. 8. Simmer for 2-3 min or until the sauce has thickened slightly. 9. Gently add the tofu cubes to the simmering sauce, being careful not to break them apart. 10. Simmer for 5-7 min or until the tofu is heated through and has absorbed the sauce. 11. Stir in soy sauce and sugar. 12. Simmer for 1 min more to combine flavors. 13. Stir in chopped green onions. 14. Serve immediately over cooked rice. 15. Garnish with additional chopped green onions and a drizzle of sesame oil (opt).

Nutritional info: 300 cal, 18g protein, 20g carbs, 18g fat, 4g fiber.

General Tso's Chicken

Yields: 4 servings **Prep time:** 20 minutes **Total time:** 40 minutes **Equipment:** Wok, spatula.

Ingredients: 1 lb boneless chicken, marinade (egg white, soy sauce, etc.), batter (cornstarch, flour, etc.), 1/4 cup oil, garlic, ginger, chilies/flakes, green onions, sauce (broth, soy sauce, etc.).

Instructions: 1. Marinate chicken for at least 15 min. 2. Coat in batter. 3. Heat vegetable oil in a wok over medium-high heat. 4. Add coated chicken pieces and fry for 3-4 min per side or until golden brown and cooked through. 5. Fry aromatics and chilies in a wok. 6. Pour chicken broth, soy sauce, rice vinegar, brown sugar, and sesame oil into the wok. 7. Bring to a simmer and cook for 1-2 min or until the sauce has thickened. 8. Return chicken and white onions. 9. Cook. 10. Garnish and serve over rice.

Nutritional info: 450-550 cal, 35g protein, 50g carbs, 15-25g fat, 2g fiber.

Sweet and Sour Pork

Yields: 4 servings **Prep time:** 15 minutes **Total time:** 35-40 minutes

Equipment: Wok, spatula, thermometer (optional).

Ingredients: 1 lb pork, marinade (soy sauce, etc.), batter (if deep-frying), 1/4 cup oil, 1/2 onion, 2 bell peppers, garlic, ginger, 1 can pineapple chunks (reserve juice), 1/2 cup juice, 1/4 cup vinegar, 2 tbsp ketchup & soy sauce, 1/4 cup sugar, 1 tbsp cornstarch, 1/4 cup water.

Instructions: 1. Combine pork with soy sauce, rice vinegar, cornstarch, salt, and pepper. 2. Toss to coat and marinate for at least 15 min. 3. (Opt) Dredge pork in a mixture of cornstarch and flour before frying. 4. Heat vegetable oil in a wok over medium-high heat. 5. Add pork and fry for 3-4 min per side or until golden brown and cooked through. 6. Remove. 7. In the same wok, add onion, bell peppers, garlic, and ginger. 8. Stir-fry for 3-4 min or until veggies are tender-crisp. 9. Add pineapple juice, rice vinegar, soy sauce, sugar, and cornstarch to the wok. 10. Stir to combine. 11. Bring to a simmer and cook for 1-2 min or until the sauce has thickened. 12. Return cooked pork and pineapple chunks to the wok. 13. Toss to coat in the sauce. 14. Cook for 1-2 min more or until heated through. 15. Serve over rice.

Nutritional info: 450-550 cal, 25g protein, 45-55g carbs, 15-25g fat, 2g fiber.

Chow Mein

Yields: 4 servings **Prep time:** 15 minutes **Total time:** 30 minutes **Equipment:** Wok, spatula.

Ingredients: 8oz dried/12oz fresh chow mein noodles, 1 lb chicken/shrimp or 8oz tofu, 2 tbsp oil, 3 minced garlic, 1 tbsp ginger, 1/2 onion, 1 cup cabbage, 1 carrot, 1/2 cup mushrooms, 1/4 cup celery, bean sprouts (opt), 1/4 cup broth, 2 tbsp soy sauce/tamari, 1 tbsp oyster sauce, 1 tsp sesame oil, 1 tsp sugar, 1/4 tsp pepper, 1 tbsp cornstarch, 2 tbsp water, green onions.

Instructions: 1. Cook/prep noodles and toss with oil. 2. Stir-fry protein in 1 tbsp hot oil until cooked. 3. Remove. 4. Fry garlic and ginger until fragrant. 5. Add veggies and stir-fry until veggies are tender-crisp. 6. Add noodles, water/broth (if needed), and sauce. 7. Toss and cook. 8. Return protein. 9. Garnish and serve.

Nutritional info: 450-500 cal, 20-25g protein, 50-60g carbs, 15-20g fat, 4g fiber.

Spring Rolls

Yields: 12 spring rolls (4 servings) **Prep time:** 20 minutes **Total time:** 35 minutes

Equipment: Wok, spatula, thermometer, slotted spoon, bowl with water.

Ingredients: Filling: 1 tbsp oil, 1/2 cup shredded cabbage & carrots, 1/4 cup mushrooms, bean sprouts, 2 garlic cloves, 1 tbsp ginger, salt, pepper. Wrappers: 12 wrappers. Deep Frying: Oil. Dipping Sauce (opt): soy sauce, vinegar, sesame oil, chili garlic sauce.

Instructions: 1. Heat oil in a wok over medium-high heat. 2. Add garlic and ginger and stir-fry for 30 sec until fragrant. 3. Add shredded cabbage, carrots, mushrooms, and bean sprouts. 4. Stir-fry for 3-5 min or until veggies are tender-crisp. 5. Season with salt and pepper to taste. 6. Cool. 7. Place filling on the wrapper, fold & seal with water. 8. Heat oil to 350°F. 9. Fry rolls until golden brown. 10. Serve with sauce (opt).

Nutritional info (3 rolls): 200 cal, 4g protein, 25g carbs, 10g fat, 2g fiber.

Wonton Soup

Yields: 4 servings **Prep time:** 30 minutes **Total time:** 45 minutes **Equipment:** Wok, spatula, steamer.

Ingredients: Filling: 1/2 lb ground pork, 1/4 cup chopped shrimp (opt), water chestnuts, 2 green onions, garlic, ginger, 1 tbsp soy sauce, sesame oil, salt, pepper. Wrappers: 24. Soup: 6 cups broth, ginger, garlic, salt, pepper. Pan-fry (opt): 1 tbsp oil. Garnish: green onions, cilantro (opt).

Instructions: 1. Combine ground pork, shrimp (opt), water chestnuts, green onions, garlic, ginger, soy sauce, sesame oil, salt, and pepper. 2. Mix well. 3. Place a wonton wrapper on a clean surface with one corner pointing towards you. 4. Place a small amount of filling in the center of the wrapper. 5. Fold the bottom corner over the filling, then fold in the sides. 6. Roll up the wrapper tightly, moistening the top corner with water to seal. 7. Repeat with the remaining wrappers. 8. Simmer broth, aromatics, seasonings in wok. 9. (Opt) Pan-fry wontons. 10. Steam wontons until cooked. 11. Ladle soup and add wontons. 12. Garnish and serve.

Nutritional info: 350 cal, 20g protein, 35g carbs, 15g fat, 2g fiber.

Hot and Sour Soup

Yields: 4 servings **Prep time:** 15 minutes **Total time:** 30 minutes **Equipment:** Wok, spatula.

Ingredients: Tofu: 4 oz tofu, 1 tbsp cornstarch. Stir-fry: 2 tbsp oil, garlic, ginger, red pepper flakes (opt), veggies (wood ear & shiitake mushrooms, bamboo shoots). Soup: 6 cups broth, 2 tbsp soy sauce, 2 tbsp vinegar, sesame oil, pepper, salt, carrot, bamboo shoots. Thickener: cornstarch, water. Egg drop: 2 eggs, sesame oil. Garnish: green onions, cilantro.

Instructions: 1. Press the tofu between paper towels for 15-20 min to remove excess moisture. 2. Cut tofu into cubes. 3. Toss with cornstarch (opt). 4. Heat oil in a wok over medium-high heat. 5. Add garlic, ginger, and red pepper flakes (opt). 6. Stir-fry until fragrant. 7. Add sliced wood ear mushrooms, shiitake mushrooms, and bamboo shoots. 8. Stir-fry until softened. 9. Add broth, sauces, pepper. 10. Simmer. 11. Add carrots and bamboo shoots and simmer. 12. Thicken with slurry. 13. Drizzle eggs. 14. Add tofu mix. 15. Garnish and serve.

Nutritional info: 280 cal, 15g protein, 25g carbs, 12g fat, 4g fiber.

Egg Drop Soup

Yields: 4 servings **Prep time:** 5 minutes **Total time:** 15 minutes **Equipment:** Wok, spatula, bowl.

Ingredients: Broth: 6 cups chicken/veggie broth, ginger, green onions (white parts). Egg Mixture: 2 eggs, 1 tbsp cornstarch, 1/4 tsp salt, pepper. Seasonings: 1 tbsp soy sauce/tamari, 1/2 tsp sesame oil. Garnish (opt): green onions (green parts), sesame oil.

Instructions: 1. Simmer broth with ginger and onions for 5 min. 2. Whisk egg mixture. 3. Remove aromatics from broth. 4. Drizzle egg mixture into simmering broth, stirring. 5. Add soy sauce, sesame oil, season. 6. Garnish and serve hot.

Nutritional info: 100 cal, 6g protein, 5g carbs, 6g fat, 0g fiber.

Thai Cuisine

Pad Thai

Yields: 2 servings **Prep time:** 15 minutes **Total time:** 30 minutes **Equipment:** Wok, spatula.

Ingredients: 8oz rice noodles, protein (shrimp/tofu/chicken), 2 tbsp oil, 2 minced garlic, 1 shallot, 1/2 bell pepper, 1/4 cup green onions & peanuts, 2 eggs, 2 cups bean sprouts, 3 tbsp tamarind paste, 2 tbsp fish sauce, 2 tbsp brown sugar, 1 tbsp lime juice, 1/2 tsp red pepper flakes, lime wedges, cilantro, peanuts.

Instructions: 1. Soak noodles. 2. Whisk together tamarind paste, fish sauce, brown sugar, lime juice, and red pepper flakes. 3. Heat 1 tbsp oil in a wok over medium-high heat. 4. Add shrimp, tofu, or chicken and cook until cooked through. 5. Remove. 6. Fry garlic and shallot. 7. Add pepper. 8. Add noodles, sauce, cook. 9. Add protein, sprouts, onions. 10. Scramble eggs. 11. Garnish and serve.

Nutritional info: 550 cal, 20g protein, 75g carbs, 20g fat, 4g fiber.

Wok-Fired Drunken Noodles (Pad Kee Mao)

Yields: 2 servings **Prep time:** 10 minutes **Total time:** 25 minutes **Equipment:** Wok, spatula.

Ingredients: 8oz wide rice noodles, 1/2 lb chicken/beef/pork or 8oz tofu, 2 tbsp oil, 3-4 minced garlic, 2-4 Thai chilies, 1/2 onion, 1/2 bell pepper, 1/2 cup mushrooms, 2 cups Thai basil, 1/4 cup green onions, 2 tbsp soy sauce, 1 tbsp fish sauce, dark soy sauce, oyster sauce, 1 tbsp brown sugar, 1/4 cup water.

Instructions: 1. Soak noodles. 2. Combine sauce. 3. Fry protein in 1 tbsp hot oil. 4. Remove. 5. Fry garlic and chilies for 2-3 min or until softened. 6. Add onion, pepper, mushrooms. 7. Add sauce and noodles and toss until softened. 8. Return protein; add basil and onions. 9. Serve hot.

Nutritional info: 500 cal, 25g protein, 65g carbs, 15g fat, 4g fiber.

Green Curry

Yields: 4 servings **Prep time:** 15 minutes **Total time:** 35 minutes **Equipment:** Wok, spatula.

Ingredients: 1 lb boneless chicken, 1/2 tsp salt, 1/4 tsp pepper, 2 tbsp oil, 2 tbsp green curry paste, 1 can coconut milk, 1/2 cup broth, 1/4 cup bamboo shoots, 1/2 red bell pepper, 1/2 cup broccoli, 1/4 cup snow peas, 1/2 cup Thai basil, 1 lime (juiced), Thai basil & lime wedges (garnish).

Instructions: 1. Chop veggies. 2. Fry curry paste in 1 tbsp oil. 3. Add coconut milk, broth, simmer. 4. Season & add chicken, cook. 5. Add veggies and cook until tender. 6. Add basil, lime juice. 7. Serve with rice, garnish.

Nutritional info: 450 cal, 25g protein, 30g carbs, 25g fat, 4g fiber.

Red Curry

Yields: 4 servings **Prep time:** 15 minutes **Total time:** 35 minutes **Equipment:** Wok, spatula.

Ingredients: 1 lb boneless chicken, 1/2 tsp salt, 1/4 tsp pepper, 2 tbsp oil, 2 tbsp red curry paste, 1 can coconut milk, 1/2 cup broth, 1/4 cup bamboo shoots, 1/2 red bell pepper, 1/2 cup broccoli, 1/4 cup snow peas, 1/2 cup Thai basil, 1 lime (juiced), Thai basil & lime wedges (garnish).

Instructions: 1. Chop veggies. 2. Fry curry paste in 1 tbsp oil. 3. Add coconut milk, broth, simmer. 4. Season & add chicken, cook. 5. Add veggies and cook until tender. 6. Add basil, lime juice. 7. Serve with rice, garnish.

Nutritional info: 450 cal, 25g protein, 30g carbs, 25g fat, 4g fiber.

Panang Curry

Yields: 4 servings **Prep time:** 15 minutes **Total time:** 35 minutes **Equipment:** Wok, spatula.

Ingredients: 1 lb boneless chicken, 1/2 tsp salt, 1/4 tsp pepper, 2 tbsp oil, 1/4 cup panang curry paste, 1 can coconut milk, 1/2 cup broth, 1/4 cup bamboo shoots, 1/2 red bell pepper, 1/2 cup broccoli, 1/4 cup snow peas, 1/2 cup Thai basil, 1 lime (juiced), 2 minced garlic cloves, 1 tbsp ginger, 2 kaffir lime leaves (opt), 2 tbsp fish sauce, 1 tbsp brown sugar, chopped peanuts (opt).

Instructions: 1. Chop veggies. 2. Fry garlic, ginger, lime leaves (opt) in 1 tbsp oil. 3. Add curry paste, fry. 4. Add milk, broth, simmer. 5. Season & add chicken, cook. 6. Add veggies and cook until tender. 7. Add fish sauce, sugar. 8. Add basil, lime juice. 9. Serve with rice, garnish with peanuts & basil (opt).

Nutritional info: 500 cal, 25g protein, 35g carbs, 30g fat, 4g fiber.

Pad See Ew

Yields: 2 servings **Prep time:** 10 minutes **Total time:** 25 minutes **Equipment:** Wok, spatula.

Ingredients: 8 oz wide rice noodles, protein (chicken/beef/pork/tofu), 2 tbsp oil, 2 minced garlic, 1 egg, 4-5 cups Chinese broccoli, sauce (2 tbsp dark soy sauce, 1 tbsp soy sauce, 1 tbsp oyster sauce, 1 tbsp vinegar, 1 tsp sugar, 1/4 tsp pepper), garnish (opt).

Instructions: 1. Soak noodles. 2. Fry protein in 1 tbsp hot oil. 3. Remove. 4. Fry garlic for 30 sec or until fragrant. 5. Add broccoli and stir-fry for 2-3 min or until slightly tender-crisp. 6. Add noodles and sauce and toss until softened. 7. Return protein. 8. Scramble egg in the center. 9. Garnish and serve.

Nutritional info: 450-500 cal, 15-25g protein, 60g carbs, 15-20g fat, 4g fiber.

Tom Yum Soup

Yields: 4 servings **Prep time:** 15 minutes **Total time:** 30 minutes **Equipment:** Wok, spatula.

Ingredients: 2 lemongrass stalks, 4 galangal/ginger slices, 4-6 kaffir lime leaves, 2-4 Thai chilies, 4 sliced shallots, 2 tbsp fish sauce, 1 tbsp lime juice, 4 cups broth, 1 can mushrooms (opt), 1/2 cup chopped tomatoes, 1 lb shrimp/chicken/tofu, chopped cilantro, lime wedges, chili oil (opt).

Instructions: 1. Bruise lemongrass stalks, galangal or ginger slices, and kaffir lime leaves. 2. Heat oil in a wok over medium-high heat. 3. Add bruised lemongrass, galangal or ginger, kaffir lime leaves, and Thai chili peppers. 4. Stir-fry for 30 sec or until fragrant. 5. Pour in chicken broth, fish sauce, and lime juice. 6. Bring to a simmer and cook for 2-3 min. 7. Add protein & mushrooms (opt), and cook for 2-3 min more. 8. Add tomatoes and simmer for 1-2 min or until the tomatoes have softened. 9. Serve, garnish with cilantro, lime, chili oil (opt).

Nutritional info: 250 cal, 20g protein, 15g carbs, 10g fat, 2g fiber.

Mango Sticky Rice (Khao Niao Mamuang)

Yields: 4 servings **Prep time:** 15 minutes **Total time:** 40 minutes (plus 4 hours soaking time for rice)

Equipment: Wok, steamer, spatula, saucepan

Ingredients: 1 1/2 cups sticky rice, 1 3/4 cups coconut milk, salt, 2 mangoes (sliced), 1 tbsp oil (opt), 1/2 cup coconut milk, 1 tbsp sugar, salt, sesame seeds (opt).

Instructions: 1. Rinse sticky rice until water runs clear. 2. Soak in cold water for at least 4 hours. 3. Drain. 4. Place soaked rice in a steamer basket. 5. Steam over boiling water for 20-25 min or until tender and slightly sticky. 6. Heat 1/2 cup coconut milk, sugar, salt until thickened. 7. (Opt) Fry mango in 1/4 cup coconut milk & oil. 8. Mix rice with the remaining coconut milk. 9. Top with mango, drizzle sauce, garnish with seeds.

Nutritional info: 450 cal, 5g protein, 80g carbs, 15g fat, 2g fiber.

Chicken Satay

Yields: 4 servings **Prep time:** 20 minutes **Total time:** 30 minutes (including marinating time)

Equipment: Wok, spatula, skewers.

Ingredients: 1 lb boneless chicken (cut into strips), 1/4 cup coconut milk, 2 tbsp soy sauce/tamari, 1 tbsp fish sauce & brown sugar, 1 tbsp curry powder, 1 tsp turmeric powder, 1/2 tsp ground cumin 1/4 tsp cayenne pepper (opt), 2 tbsp oil, 1/2 red onion, 1 bell pepper, cilantro, 1/2 cup peanut butter, 1/4 cup coconut milk, 2 tbsp soy sauce, 1 tbsp lime juice, 1 tsp chili garlic sauce/sriracha, cilantro.

Instructions: 1. Combine chicken strips with coconut milk, soy sauce, fish sauce, brown sugar, curry powder, turmeric powder, and cayenne pepper (opt). 2. Toss to coat and marinate for at least 15 min. 3. Thread marinated chicken onto skewers. 4. Grill or sauté chicken skewers over medium-high heat for 3-4 min per side or until cooked through. 5. In a wok, heat oil over medium-high heat. 6. Add onion and bell pepper and stir-fry for 2-3 min or until softened. 7. In a small saucepan, combine peanut butter, coconut milk, soy sauce, lime juice, and chili garlic sauce. 8. Heat over low heat, stirring constantly, until smooth and combined. 9. Serve chicken and veggies with sauce & cilantro garnish.

Nutritional info (without sauce): 350 cal, 30g protein, 15g carbs, 18g fat, 2g fiber.

Papaya Salad (Som Tum)

Yields: 4 servings **Prep time:** 20 minutes **Total time:** 25 minutes

Equipment: Wok, spatula, mortar & pestle (optional).

Ingredients: 1 green papaya (shredded), 2 cups bean sprouts, tomatoes (halved), peanuts (chopped), cilantro (chopped), 1 tbsp oil, garlic (sliced), Thai chilies (sliced), 2 tbsp fish sauce, 2 tbsp lime juice, 1 tbsp palm/brown sugar, tamarind paste (opt).

Instructions: 1. Shred green papaya. 2. Chop tomatoes, garlic, and chili peppers. 3. Heat oil in a wok over medium-high heat. 4. Add minced garlic and chili peppers. 5. Stir-fry for 30 sec or until fragrant. 6. (Opt) Place shredded papaya, tomatoes, and peanuts in a mortar and pestle. 7. Pound gently to bruise the ingredients and release their flavors. 8. In a large bowl, combine shredded papaya, bean sprouts, tomatoes, sautéed garlic and chili peppers, fish sauce, lime juice, palm sugar or brown sugar, and tamarind paste (opt). 9. Toss to combine. 10. Garnish with chopped peanuts and cilantro. 11. Serve.

Nutritional info: 200 cal, 4g protein, 20g carbs, 12g fat, 4g fiber.

Korean Cuisine

Bulgogi
Yields: 4 servings **Prep time:** 20 minutes **Total time:** 35 minutes (including marinating)

Equipment: Wok, spatula.

Ingredients: 1 lb ribeye/sirloin, 1/4 cup soy sauce, 2 tbsp mirin, 2 tbsp brown sugar, 1 tbsp sesame oil, 2 minced garlic, 1 tbsp ginger, 1/4 cup green onions, 1/4 tsp pepper, 1 tbsp oil, 1/2 onion, 1/2 cup mushrooms (opt), 1/4 cup carrots (opt), sesame seeds (opt).

Instructions: 1. Combine beef with marinade ingredients, and marinate for at least 15 min. 2. Heat oil in a wok over medium-high heat. 3. Add marinated beef and cook in batches, stirring frequently, until browned. 4. Remove. 5. Fry veggies (opt) until softened. 6. Return beef and any remaining marinade. 7. Cook for 1-2 min or until heated through and the sauce has thickened. 8. Garnish and serve.

Nutritional info: 400 cal, 30g protein, 20g carbs, 25g fat, 2g fiber.

Bibimbap
Yields: 4 servings **Prep time:** 20 minutes **Total time:** 40 minutes **Equipment:** Wok, spatula.

Ingredients: 2 cups cooked rice, 2 tbsp oil, protein (1/2 lb beef or tofu), veggies (spinach, bean sprouts, carrots, zucchini, mushrooms), garlic, gochujang, soy sauce/tamari, sesame oil, 1 egg (opt), kimchi (opt), sesame seeds (opt).

Instructions: 1. Prep veggies & protein. 2. Marinate beef (opt). 3. Stir-fry beef/tofu in 1 tbsp oil. 4. Remove. 5. Fry garlic in remaining oil for 30 sec or until fragrant. 6. Add veggies and stir-fry for 2-3 min or until tender-crisp. 7. Add rice and fry. 8. Assemble in bowls: rice, beef/tofu, veggies, egg (opt). 9. Serve with gochujang, soy sauce, sesame oil, kimchi & seeds (opt).

Nutritional info: 400-500 cal, 15-25g protein, 50-60g carbs, 15-20g fat, 3-5g fiber.

Japchae (Korean Glass Noodle Stir-fry)
Yields: 4 servings **Prep time:** 20 minutes **Total time:** 40 minutes **Equipment:** Wok, spatula.

Ingredients: 8oz dangmyeon noodles, 1/2 lb beef, 1 tbsp soy sauce, 1 tsp sugar, garlic, pepper, sesame oil, 2 tbsp oil, 2 garlic cloves, 1 onion, 1 carrot, bell peppers, mushrooms (opt), 5oz spinach, 3 tbsp soy sauce, 1 tbsp honey/sugar, 1 tsp sesame oil, 1/4 tsp pepper, sesame seeds, egg omelet (opt).

Instructions: 1. Soak noodles, and marinate beef for at least 15 min. 2. Fry beef in 1 tbsp hot oil. 3. Remove. 4. Fry garlic for 30 sec or until fragrant. 5. Add onion, carrots, peppers, and mushrooms (opt). 6. Stir-fry for 2-3 min or until softened. 7. Add spinach and sauce. 8. Add noodles and beef. 9. Toss until heated. 10. Garnish and serve.

Nutritional info: 400 cal, 20g protein, 50g carbs, 15g fat, 3g fiber.

Kimchi Fried Rice (Kimchi Bokkeumbap)

Yields: 4 servings **Prep time:** 10 minutes **Total time:** 25 minutes **Equipment:** Wok, spatula.

Ingredients: 3 cups cooked rice, 1 cup chopped kimchi, 2 tbsp kimchi juice, 1 tbsp gochujang (opt), 2 tbsp oil, 4 minced garlic cloves, 1/2 cup chopped onion, 1/4 cup diced carrots & chopped green onions (separated), 1/2 cup pork belly/bacon (opt), 1 tbsp soy sauce/tamari, 1/2 tsp sesame oil, salt, pepper, 1 fried egg (opt), kimchi (opt), sesame seeds (opt).

Instructions: 1. Prep veggies. 2. Heat 1 tbsp oil in a wok over medium-high heat. 3. Add chopped kimchi and kimchi juice. 4. Stir-fry for 2-3 min or until heated through. 5. Add oil, garlic, onion, carrots, stir-fry for 2-3 min or until softened. 6. Add pork/bacon (opt), cook. 7. Add cooked rice to the wok and increase heat to high. 8. Stir-fry vigorously for 3-5 min or until the rice is coated in the kimchi and vegetable mixture and becomes slightly crispy. 9. Add soy sauce, sesame oil, salt, pepper, and white onions. 10. Serve, top with egg, kimchi, and seeds (opt).

Nutritional info (without egg & toppings): 350 kcal, 8g protein, 55g carbs, 12g fat, 3g fiber.

Dakgalbi (Spicy Stir-fried Chicken)

Yields: 4 servings **Prep time:** 20 minutes **Total time:** 40 minutes (including marinating)

Equipment: Wok, spatula.

Ingredients: 1 lb boneless chicken, 2 tbsp gochujang, 2 tbsp soy sauce/tamari, 1 tbsp rice wine/mirin, 1 tbsp honey/sugar, 1 tsp sesame oil, 1/2 tsp ginger, 2 minced garlic cloves, 2 tbsp oil, 1 onion, 2 cups cabbage, 1 cup sweet potato, 1/2 cup carrots, 1/4 cup green onions, 2-3 chilies (opt), 1/4 cup rice cakes (opt), sesame seeds, rice.

Instructions: 1. Marinate chicken in all marinade ingredients for at least 15 min. 2. Stir-fry in hot oil until cooked. 3. Remove. 4. Stir-fry onion, cabbage, sweet potato, carrots, onions, and chilies (opt) for 3-4 min or until veggies are softened. 5. Add rice cakes (opt) in the last 2 min. 6. Return chicken and cook. 7. Serve with rice and garnish with sesame seeds.

Nutritional info: 450 cal, 30g protein, 40g carbs, 20g fat, 4g fiber.

Tteokbokki (Spicy Rice Cakes)

Yields: 2 servings **Prep time:** 10 minutes **Total time:** 25-35 minutes **Equipment:** Wok, spatula.

Ingredients: 12oz rice cakes, 1 tbsp oil, 1/4 cup onion, 2 minced garlic, 1/2 cup fish cakes, 1/4 cup green onions, 2 tbsp gochujang, 1 tbsp soy sauce, 1 tbsp sugar, 1/4 tsp fish sauce (opt), 1 cup water/broth, sesame seeds, green onions, hard-boiled egg (opt).

Instructions: 1. Prep veggies. 2. Heat oil in a wok over medium-high heat. 3. Add minced garlic and onion. 4. Stir-fry for 30 sec or until fragrant. 5. Add fish cakes and stir-fry for 2-3 min or until heated through. 6. Add gochujang, soy sauce, sugar, fish sauce (opt), water/broth, simmer. 7. Add rice cakes and cook until tender & sauce thickens. 8. Garnish and serve hot.

Nutritional info: 400 cal, 12g protein, 60g carbs, 10g fat, 2g fiber.

Kimchi Jjigae (Kimchi Stew)

Yields: 4 servings **Prep time:** 10 minutes **Total time:** 35 minutes **Equipment:** Wok, spatula.

Ingredients: 1 tbsp oil, 1/2 lb pork belly (sliced), 1 cup kimchi (chopped), 1/4 cup kimchi juice, 1/2 onion (sliced), 2 minced garlic, 1 tbsp gochugaru, 4 cups broth, 1/2 cup tofu (cubed), 1/4 cup green onions (sliced), 1 tbsp doenjang (opt), 1/4 cup scallions (opt), 1/4 cup zucchini/mushrooms (opt).

Instructions: 1. Heat oil in a wok over medium-high heat. 2. Add pork belly and cook until browned. 3. Remove. 4. In the same wok, add chopped kimchi and kimchi juice. 5. Stir-fry for 2-3 min or until heated through. 6. Add diced onion and minced garlic. 7. Stir-fry for 30 sec or until fragrant. 8. Add gochugaru and stir-fry for another 30 sec. 9. Add broth, tofu, doenjang (opt). 10. Boil, then simmer for 15 min. 11. Return cooked pork belly to the wok. 12. Add cubed tofu and simmer for 5-7 min or until tofu is heated through. 13. During the last 5 min of simmering, add sliced zucchini or mushrooms (opt). 14. Garnish with onions and serve with rice.

Nutritional info: 350 cal, 20g protein, 30g carbs, 15g fat, 4g fiber.

Doenjang Jjigae (Soybean Paste Stew)

Yields: 4 servings **Prep time:** 15 minutes **Total time:** 40 minutes **Equipment:** Wok, spatula.

Ingredients: Protein (1/2 lb pork belly/tofu/seafood), 1 tbsp oil, 2 minced garlic, 1 tbsp doenjang, 1 tsp gochugaru, 1/2 onion, 1/2 zucchini, 1/2 cup mushrooms, green onions (separated), 4 cups anchovy broth/water, 1/4 cup potato & zucchini, 1/4 cup kimchi (opt), garnish (green onions, chili pepper).

Instructions: 1. Prep veggies. 2. If using anchovies, simmer in water for 15 min strain. 3. Heat oil in a wok over medium heat. 4. Add garlic and doenjang, stir-fry for 1 min until fragrant. 5. Add gochugaru and stir for another 30 sec. 6. Add onion, zucchini, mushrooms, and white onions. 7. Stir-fry for 3-4 min until veggies are softened. 8. Add broth, potatoes, zucchini, kimchi (opt). 9. Simmer until potatoes are tender. 10. Add protein and cook. 11. Garnish and serve with rice.

Nutritional info: 350-450 cal, 15-25g protein, 30-40g carbs, 15-25g fat, 4g fiber.

Korean Fried Chicken

Yields: 4 servings **Prep time:** 20 minutes **Total time:** 40-45 minutes (including marinating)

Equipment: Wok, spatula, thermometer.

Ingredients: 1 lb boneless chicken, 1 tbsp soy sauce, 1 tsp ginger, 2 garlic cloves, 1/4 tsp pepper, 1/2 cup flour & cornstarch, 1/4 tsp baking powder & salt, water, oil for frying, 2 tbsp gochujang, 2 tbsp honey/corn syrup, 1 tbsp soy sauce & rice vinegar, 1/2 tsp sesame oil, 1 garlic clove, 1/4 tsp ginger, garnish (sesame seeds, green onions, red pepper flakes) (opt).

Instructions: 1. Marinate chicken for at least 15 min. 2. Make a batter by whisking flour, cornstarch, baking powder, salt, and water. 3. Heat sauce in a saucepan until thickened. 4. Heat oil to 350°F. 5. Coat chicken in batter and deep-fry until golden brown. 6. Toss fried chicken with sauce in a wok. 7. Garnish and serve hot.

Nutritional info: 500-600 cal, 30g protein, 40-50g carbs, 25-35g fat, 2g fiber.

Haemul Pajeon (Seafood Pancake)

Yields: 4 servings **Prep time:** 15 minutes **Total time:** 30 minutes **Equipment:** Wok, spatula.

Ingredients: 1 cup pancake mix/flour, 1 cup water, 1 egg, 1/2 cup shrimp, 1/4 cup squid/calamari, mussels/clams (opt), green onions, carrots, onion, chilies/flakes, 2-3 tbsp oil, dipping sauce (soy sauce, vinegar, sesame oil), green onions, sesame seeds (opt).

Instructions: 1. Whisk together pancake mix (or flour), water, and egg until smooth, rest for 5 min. 2. Add seafood, veggies, chilies. 3. Heat oil in a wok over medium-high heat. 4. Pour about 1/2 cup of batter into the hot skillet. 5. Cook for 2-3 min or until the edges are set and the bottom is golden brown. 6. Flip and cook for another 2-3 min or until the other side is golden brown. 7. Repeat with the remaining batter. 8. Slice, serve with sauce and garnish.

Nutritional info (1/4): 350 cal, 15g protein, 40g carbs, 15g fat, 2g fiber.

Mandu (Korean Dumplings)

Yields: Approximately 30 dumplings (6 servings) **Prep time:** 30 minutes **Total time:** 45 minutes
Equipment: Wok, spatula, lid.

Ingredients: 30 wrappers, Filling (choose one or mix): Beef: 1/2 lb ground beef, kimchi, tofu, onion, garlic, ginger, soy sauce, sesame oil, pepper. Pork & Kimchi: 1/2 lb ground pork, kimchi, onion, garlic, ginger, soy sauce, sesame oil, pepper. 1 tbsp oil, 1/2 cup water. Dipping Sauce: soy sauce, vinegar, sesame oil, red pepper flakes.

Instructions: 1. Combine filling ingredients. 2. Place filling on the wrapper, moisten edges, and pleat to seal. 3. Pan-fry in oil for 2-3 min per side or until golden brown. 4. Add 1/2 cup of water to the wok. 5. Cover and steam for 5-7 min or until dumplings are cooked through and the filling is heated. 6. Serve with dipping sauce.

Nutritional info (6 dumplings): Beef: 350 cal, 18g protein, 25g carbs, 20g fat, 2g fiber. Pork & Kimchi: 400 cal, 20g protein, 30g carbs, 22g fat, 3g fiber.

Japanese Cuisine

Yakisoba

Yields: 4 servings **Prep time:** 15 minutes **Total time:** 30 minutes **Equipment:** Wok, spatula.

Ingredients: 12oz fresh/8oz dried yakisoba noodles, 1/2 lb protein (pork/chicken/beef/shrimp), 2 tbsp oil, 3 minced garlic, 1 onion, 1 carrot, mushrooms (opt), 3 cups cabbage, 3 tbsp Worcestershire sauce, 2 tbsp ketchup, 2 tbsp soy sauce/tamari, 1 tbsp oyster sauce, 1 tsp sugar, 1/4 tsp pepper, garnish (opt).

Instructions: 1. Cook/prep noodles and toss with oil. 2. Fry protein in 1 tbsp hot oil. 3. Remove. 4. Fry garlic for 30 sec or until fragrant. 5. Add onion, carrots, and mushrooms (opt). 6. Add cabbage. 7. Stir-fry for 2-3 min or until veggies are tender-crisp. 8. Add noodles, sauce, toss. 9. Return protein. 10. Garnish and serve.

Nutritional info: 450-550 cal, 15-25g protein, 60-70g carbs, 15-25g fat, 3-5g fiber.

Teriyaki Chicken

Yields: 4 servings **Prep time:** 15 minutes **Total time:** 30-35 minutes **Equipment:** Wok/skillet, spatula.

Ingredients: 1 lb boneless chicken, 2 tbsp soy sauce/tamari, 1 tbsp cornstarch, 1 tsp sesame oil, 2 tbsp oil, 2 minced garlic, 1 tbsp ginger, 1/2 onion, 1 bell pepper (opt), 1/2 cup broccoli (opt), 1/4 cup soy sauce/tamari, 1/4 cup mirin, 1/4 cup sake (opt), 2 tbsp honey/sugar, 1/4 tsp ginger, sesame seeds, green onions (opt).

Instructions: 1. Marinate chicken for at least 15 min. 2. Whisk sauce ingredients. 3. Heat oil in a wok or skillet over medium-high heat. 4. Add marinated chicken and cook for 3-4 min per side or until cooked through and golden brown. 5. Remove. 6. Fry veggies (opt). 7. Add sauce and simmer. 8. Return chicken and veggies (opt). 9. Cook. 10. Garnish and serve.

Nutritional info: 400-450 cal, 30g protein, 20-25g carbs, 15-20g fat, 2g fiber.

Chicken Katsu

Yields: 4 servings **Prep time:** 15 minutes **Total time:** 30 minutes

Equipment: Wok, spatula, thermometer, slotted spoon.

Ingredients: 4 chicken breasts, salt, pepper, 1/2 cup flour, 1 egg, 1 cup panko, oil for frying, tonkatsu sauce (opt), rice, cabbage.

Instructions: 1. Pound chicken breasts to an even thickness. 2. Season with salt and pepper. 3. Set up a breading station with three shallow dishes: one with flour, one with beaten egg, and one with panko bread crumbs. 4. Coat chicken in flour, egg, panko. 5. Heat oil to 350°F. 6. Fry chicken until golden brown. 7. Drain. 8. Slice & serve over rice with cabbage & sauce (opt).

Nutritional info: 500 cal, 30g protein, 40g carbs, 25g fat, 2g fiber.

Gyoza

Yields: 20-24 gyoza (4-6 servings) **Prep time:** 30 minutes **Total time:** 45 minutes

Equipment: Wok, spatula, lid.

Ingredients: 20-24 wrappers, 1/2 lb ground pork, 1/2 cup chopped Napa cabbage, 1/4 cup grated carrot, 2 green onions, 2 garlic cloves, 1 tbsp ginger, 2 tbsp soy sauce, 1 tbsp sesame oil, 1/2 tsp sugar, 1/4 tsp pepper & salt, 1 tbsp oil, 1/2 cup water, dipping sauce (soy sauce, vinegar, chili oil), sesame seeds (opt).

Instructions: 1. Combine filling ingredients. 2 Place a wonton wrapper on a clean surface with one corner pointing towards you. 3. Place a small amount of filling in the center of the wrapper. 4. Fold the bottom corner over the filling, then fold in the sides. 5. Roll up the wrapper tightly, moistening the top corner with water to seal. 6. Repeat with the remaining wrappers. 7. Pan-fry in oil until golden. 8. Add 1/2 cup of water and steam until cooked. 9. Crisp up bottoms. 10. Serve with dipping sauce and garnish.

Nutritional info (6 gyoza): 350 cal, 15g protein, 30g carbs, 18g fat, 2g fiber.

Ramen

Yields: 2 servings **Prep time:** 15 minutes **Total time:** 30 minutes **Equipment:** Wok, spatula.

Ingredients: 2 packs ramen noodles, 1/2 lb protein (pork/chicken/tofu/shrimp), 1 tbsp oil, 2 garlic, 1 tbsp ginger, 1/2 onion, 1 cup mushrooms, 2 cups bok choy, 4 cups broth, 1 tbsp soy sauce/tamari, 1/2 tsp sesame oil, soft-boiled eggs, nori, green onions, sesame seeds.

Instructions: 1. Cook/prep noodles. 2. Heat oil in a wok over medium-high heat. 3. Add chicken, tofu, pork, or shrimp and cook until cooked through. 4. Remove. 5. Add minced garlic and ginger to the wok. 6. Stir-fry for 30 sec or until fragrant. 7. Add onion and mushrooms. 8. Stir-fry for 2-3 min or until softened. 9. Add bok choy and stir-fry for 1-2 min or until slightly wilted. 10. Add broth, soy sauce, sesame oil. 11. Simmer. 12. Add noodles and cook for 1-2 min or until noodles are heated through. 13. Return protein and veggies. 14. Top with egg (opt), nori, onions, and seeds. 15. Serve.

Nutritional info: 400-500 cal, 20-30g protein, 50-60g carbs, 15-20g fat, 3-5g fiber.

Udon Stir-fry

Yields: 4 servings **Prep time:** 10 minutes **Total time:** 25 minutes **Equipment:** Wok, spatula.

Ingredients: 12 oz udon noodles, protein (chicken/beef/pork/tofu), 2 tbsp oil, 3 minced garlic cloves, 1 tbsp ginger, 1/2 onion, 1 carrot, 1 cup mushrooms, 1/2 cup broccoli, 1/4 cup snow peas, 1/4 cup soy sauce/tamari, 1 tbsp mirin, 1 tsp sesame oil, 1/4 tsp pepper, 1/4 cup water, green onions, sesame seeds.

Instructions: 1. Cook noodles, drain, rinse, toss with oil. 2. Fry protein in 1 tbsp hot oil until cooked. 3. Remove. 4. Fry garlic and ginger for 30 sec or until fragrant. 5. Add veggies and stir-fry for 2-3 min or until veggies are tender-crisp. 6. Add soy sauce, mirin, sesame oil, black pepper, and water to the wok. 7. Bring to a simmer and cook for 1-2 min or until the sauce has thickened. 8. Add noodles and toss. 9. Return protein. 10. Garnish with chopped green onions and sesame seeds serve hot.

Nutritional info: 450-550 cal, 15-25g protein, 60-70g carbs, 15-20g fat, 4-5g fiber.

Sesame Ginger Soba Noodles

Yields: 4 servings **Prep time:** 10 minutes **Total time:** 25 minutes **Equipment:** Wok, spatula.

Ingredients: 12 oz soba noodles, protein (chicken/beef/pork/tofu), 2 tbsp oil, 3 minced garlic, 1 tbsp ginger, 1/2 onion, 1 carrot, 1/2 cup mushrooms, 1/4 cup snow peas, 2 green onions (separated), 1/4 cup soy sauce/tamari, 2 tbsp mirin, 1 tbsp vinegar, 1 tbsp honey/syrup, 1 tbsp sesame oil, 1/4 tsp flakes (opt), sesame seeds.

Instructions: 1. Cook noodles, drain, rinse, toss with oil. 2. Fry protein in 1 tbsp hot oil. 3. Remove. 4. Fry garlic and ginger for 30 sec or until fragrant. 5. Add veggies and stir-fry for 2-3 min or until veggies are tender-crisp. 6. In a small bowl, whisk together soy sauce, mirin, rice vinegar, honey or sugar, sesame oil, and red pepper flakes (opt). 7. Add sauce and noodles. 8. Toss. 9. Return protein. 10. Garnish and serve hot.

Nutritional info: 450-550 cal, 15-25g protein, 60-70g carbs, 15-20g fat, 4-6g fiber.

Tempura

Yields: 4 servings **Prep time:** 20 minutes **Total time:** 35 minutes

Equipment: Wok, spatula, thermometer, saucepan, slotted spoon.

Ingredients: Batter: 1 cup ice water, 1 egg, 1 cup flour. For frying: 1/2 lb shrimp (opt), 1/2 sweet potato, zucchini (sliced), mushrooms, broccoli, green beans. Deep-fry: Oil. Tentsuyu Sauce: 1 cup dashi/broth, 1/4 cup mirin & soy sauce, ginger. Garnish: daikon radish, lemon.

Instructions: 1. In a bowl, whisk together ice water, egg, and flour until smooth and slightly lumpy. 2. Let batter rest in the refrigerator for at least 30 min. 3. (Opt) Peel and devein shrimp. 4. Slice sweet potato, zucchini, mushrooms, broccoli, and green beans into bite-sized pieces. 5. Heat oil to 350°F (175°C). 6. Dip veggies and shrimp in the batter, shaking off any excess. 7. Carefully add a few pieces to the hot oil, being careful not to overcrowd the pot. 8. Fry for 2-3 min or until golden brown and crispy. 9. Remove from oil and drain on paper towels. 10. Repeat until all veggies and shrimp are fried. 11. In a small saucepan, combine dashi or chicken broth, mirin, soy sauce, and grated ginger. 12. Bring to a simmer and cook for 1-2 min or until the sauce has thickened slightly. 13. Serve tempura hot with tentsuyu sauce for dipping. 14. Garnish with grated daikon radish and lemon wedges.

Nutritional info: 400 cal, 10g protein (with shrimp), 50g carbs, 20g fat, 2g fiber.

Chicken Karaage

Yields: 4 servings **Prep time:** 20 minutes **Total time:** 35 minutes (including marinating)

Equipment: Wok, spatula, bowl, thermometer.

Ingredients: 1 lb boneless chicken thighs, marinade (soy sauce, sake/mirin, ginger, garlic, pepper), potato starch/cornstarch, oil for frying, lemon wedges, mayo, shichimi togarashi (all optional garnish).

Instructions: 1. In a bowl, combine chicken with soy sauce, mirin, ginger, garlic, and black pepper. 2. Toss to coat and marinate for at least 15 min. 3. Dredge chicken pieces in potato starch or cornstarch, shaking off any excess. 4. Heat oil in a deep fryer or large pot to 350°F (175°C). 5. Carefully add coated chicken pieces to the hot oil, being careful not to overcrowd the pot. 6. Fry for 3-4 min per side or until golden brown and crispy. 7. Remove from oil and drain on paper towels. 8. For extra crispy chicken, return fried chicken to the hot oil and fry for another 1-2 min. 9. (Opt) Double-fry for extra crispiness. 10. Serve hot with lemon wedges, mayonnaise, and shichimi togarashi (opt).

Nutritional info: 450 cal, 25g protein, 30g carbs, 25g fat, 1g fiber.

Chapter 11: Special Occasion Menus

Wok Desserts

Banana Fritters

Yields: 4 servings (about 12 fritters) **Prep time:** 10 minutes **Total time:** 20 minutes

Equipment: Wok, spatula, thermometer, bowl, slotted spoon.

Ingredients: Batter: 1 cup flour, 1/4 cup cornstarch, 1 tsp baking powder, 1/4 tsp salt, 3/4 cup water/sparkling water, sugar (opt). Fritters: 3 bananas and oil for frying. Garnish: powdered sugar, honey/syrup (opt).

Instructions: 1. In a bowl, whisk together flour, cornstarch, baking powder, salt, water or sparkling water, and sugar (opt). 2. Heat oil to 350°F. 3. Dip banana slices in the batter, shaking off any excess. 4. Add a few banana slices to the hot oil. 5. Fry until golden brown and crispy. 6. Remove from oil and drain on paper towels. 7. Dust with powdered sugar and drizzle with sweetener (opt). 8. Serve warm.

Nutritional info (3 fritters): 250 cal, 3g protein, 35g carbs, 12g fat, 2g fiber.

Fried Ice Cream

Yields: 4 servings **Prep time:** 20 minutes **Total time:** 22-23 minutes (plus freezing time)

Equipment: Wok, spatula, thermometer, baking sheet & parchment paper.

Ingredients: 1 qt vanilla ice cream, 1 cup cornflakes, 1/2 cup coconut, 1/4 cup flour, 2 eggs, 1/4 cup milk, oil for frying, honey/chocolate syrup/caramel sauce.

Instructions: 1. Scoop ice cream balls and freeze. 2. Combine cornflakes, coconut, and flour. 3. Whisk eggs & milk. 4. Coat ice cream in cornflake mix and egg mix, then cornflake mix again. 5. Freeze. 6. Heat oil to 350°F. 7. Fry each ball until golden brown. 8. Drain. 9. Serve with drizzle.

Nutritional info: 400 cal, 5g protein, 45g carbs, 25g fat, 2g fiber.

Sweet Sesame Balls (Jin Deui)

Yields: Approximately 20 sesame balls **Prep time:** 20 minutes **Total time:** 60 minutes (including resting time: 30 minutes)

Equipment: Wok, spatula, thermometer, slotted spoon.

Ingredients: Dough: 1 cup glutinous rice flour, 1/4 cup sugar, 1/2 tsp baking powder, 1/2 cup water. Filling: 1/2 cup red bean paste, 1/4 cup nuts (opt). Coating: 1 cup sesame seeds and oil for frying.

Instructions: 1. Combine dough ingredients, knead, and rest. 2. Mix filling (opt). 3. Divide dough, flatten, fill, and seal. 4. Coat in seeds. 5. Fry in 350°F oil until golden brown. 6. Drain and serve.

Nutritional info (2 balls): 200 cal, 2g protein, 30g carbs, 8g fat, 1g fiber.

Gingerbread Stir-fry

Yields: 4 servings **Prep time:** 15 minutes **Total time:** 30 minutes **Equipment:** Wok, spatula.

Ingredients: Meatballs: 1 lb ground pork, 1/2 cup panko, 1/4 cup molasses, 1 egg, 1 tbsp ginger, 1 tsp cinnamon, 1/2 tsp cloves, 1/4 tsp nutmeg, salt. Stir-fry: 2 tbsp oil, 1 onion, 2 bell peppers, 1/2 cup carrots, 2 minced garlic cloves. Sauce: 1/4 cup orange juice, 2 tbsp soy sauce/tamari, 1 tbsp honey, 1 tsp cornstarch, 2 tbsp water. Garnish (opt): pecans/walnuts.

Instructions: 1. Combine meatball ingredients and form into balls. 2. Fry in 1 tbsp hot oil until browned. 3. Remove. 4. Stir-fry veggies and garlic in the remaining oil. 5. Add orange juice, soy sauce, honey. 6. Thicken with cornstarch slurry. 7. Return meatballs and cook for 1-2 min more or until heated through. 8. Garnish with chopped pecans or walnuts (opt). 9. Serve.

Nutritional info: 450 cal, 25g protein, 40g carbs, 20g fat, 3g fiber.

Honey Glazed Apples

Yields: 4 servings **Prep time:** 5 minutes **Total time:** 15 minutes **Equipment:** Wok, bowl, spatula.

Ingredients: 2 tbsp butter, 4 apples (cored, sliced), 1/4 cup honey, 1 tbsp lemon juice, 1/4 tsp cinnamon, salt, 1/4 cup nuts (opt), rum/brandy (opt), vanilla ice cream.

Instructions: 1. Melt butter in a wok over medium heat. 2. Add sliced apples and stir-fry for 3-5 min or until softened. 3. In a small bowl, whisk together honey, lemon juice, cinnamon, and a pinch of salt. 4. Pour the honey-lemon glaze over the sautéed apples. 5. Toss to coat. 6. Cook for 1-2 min more, or until the glaze has thickened and caramelized slightly. 7. Add nuts (opt) at the last minute. 8. Deglaze with rum/brandy (opt). 9. Serve warm with ice cream (opt).

Nutritional info: 200 cal, 1g protein, 35g carbs, 7g fat, 3g fiber.

Caramelized Bananas

Yields: 2 servings **Prep time:** 5 minutes **Total time:** 15 minutes **Equipment:** Wok, spatula.

Ingredients: 2 bananas, sliced, 1 tbsp butter, 1/4 cup brown sugar, 1/2 tsp cinnamon, nutmeg, cayenne (opt), 1 tbsp rum/brandy (opt), ice cream/whipped cream (opt).

Instructions: 1. Heat butter in a wok over medium-high heat. 2. Add brown sugar and stir constantly until the sugar melts and caramelizes, turning a golden brown color. This may take 2-3 min. 3. Stir in cinnamon and nutmeg. 4. Add a pinch of cayenne pepper for a hint of spice (opt). 5. Add sliced bananas to the caramelized sugar mixture. 6. Toss to coat the bananas in the caramel. 7. Cook for 2-3 min or until the bananas are softened and caramelized. 8. If using rum or brandy, carefully add the alcohol to the pan. 9. Ignite the alcohol with a match or lighter. 10. Let the flames extinguish before continuing. 11. Serve caramelized bananas immediately, topped with vanilla ice cream or whipped cream (opt).

Nutritional info: 250 cal, 1g protein, 45g carbs, 8g fat, 2g fiber.

Apple Cinnamon Spring Rolls

Yields: 12 spring rolls (4 servings) **Prep time:** 15 minutes **Total time:** 25 minutes

Equipment: Wok, spatula, thermometer.

Ingredients: Filling: 2 tbsp butter, 4 apples (diced), 1/4 cup brown sugar, 1 tsp cinnamon, 1/4 tsp nutmeg, salt. Wrappers: 12 wrappers. Deep-Frying: Oil. Dipping Sauce (opt): caramel, ice cream, whipped cream.

Instructions: 1. Heat butter in a wok over medium heat. 2. Add diced apples and stir-fry for 3-5 min or until softened. 3. Stir in brown sugar, cinnamon, and nutmeg. 4. Cook for 1-2 min more, or until the apples are coated in the sweet and spiced mixture. 5. Cool. 6. Place a spring roll wrapper on a clean surface with one corner pointing towards you. 7. Place a small amount of apple filling in the lower center of the wrapper. 8. Fold the bottom corner over the filling, then fold in the sides. 9. Roll up the wrapper tightly, moistening the top corner with water to seal. 10. Repeat with the remaining wrappers. 11. Fry in 350°F oil until golden brown. 12. Carefully add a few spring rolls to the hot oil, being careful not to overcrowd the pot. 13. Fry for 2-3 min or until golden brown and crispy. 14. Remove from oil with a slotted spoon and drain on paper towels. 15. Serve with sauce (opt).

Nutritional info (3 rolls): 250 cal, 1g protein, 35g carbs, 12g fat, 2g fiber.

Chocolate Wontons

Yields: 12 wontons (4 servings) **Prep time:** 15 minutes **Total time:** 25 minutes

Equipment: Wok, spatula, thermometer, slotted spoon.

Ingredients: Filling: 1/2 cup chocolate chips, 1/4 cup nuts (opt), 1/4 cup marshmallow fluff/minis, salt. Wrappers: 12 wrappers. Deep-fry: Oil. Garnish (opt): powdered sugar, chocolate sauce.

Instructions: 1. Melt chocolate & fluff; add nuts & salt. 2. Cool slightly. 3. Place a wonton wrapper on a clean surface with one corner pointing towards you. 4. Place a small amount of chocolate filling in the center of the wrapper. 5. Fold the bottom corner over the filling, then fold in the sides. 6. Roll up the wrapper tightly, moistening the top corner with water to seal. 7. Repeat with the remaining wrappers. 8. Fry in 350°F oil until golden. 9. Drain. 10. Garnish and serve warm.

Nutritional info (3): 350 cal, 4g protein, 40g carbs, 18g fat, 1g fiber.

Tempura Battered Oreos

Yields: 12 Oreos (2-4 servings) **Prep time:** 10 minutes **Total time:** 50 minutes (including chill time: 30 minutes)

Equipment: Wok, spatula, thermometer, slotted spoon.

Ingredients: 12 Oreos, 1 cup flour, 2 tsp baking powder, 1/4 tsp salt, 1 cup ice water, 1 tbsp sugar, oil for frying.

Instructions: 1. Freeze Oreos. 2. Whisk batter ingredients. 3. Heat oil to 350°F. 4. Dip Oreos in batter and fry until golden brown. 5. Drain on paper towels. 6. Serve warm.

Nutritional info (3 Oreos): 350 cal, 4g protein, 45g carbs, 18g fat, 1g fiber.

Recipes for Weekend Feasts

Whole Steamed Fish with Ginger and Scallions
Yields: 2-4 servings (depending on the size of the fish) **Prep time:** 10 minutes **Total time:** 25-30 minutes

Equipment: Wok, steamer basket, spatula.

Ingredients: 1 whole fish, 1 tbsp rice wine, 1/2 tsp salt, ginger (sliced/julienned), green onions, 2 tbsp soy sauce, 1 tbsp sesame oil, 1/4 cup oil.

Instructions: 1. Prep & season fish, stuff with ginger & onions. 2. Boil water in a wok and steam fish until cooked. 3. Fry remaining ginger & onions in oil; add sauces. 4. Remove fish and discard old aromatics. 5. Pour the hot oil mixture over the fish. 6. Serve with rice.

Nutritional info: 350-450 cal, 35-45g protein, 5g carbs, 15-25g fat, 1g fiber.

Orange Beef Tenderloin
Yields: 4 servings **Prep time:** 15 minutes **Total time:** 27-30 minutes **Equipment:** Wok, spatula.

Ingredients: 1 lb beef tenderloin (cubed), 1 tbsp soy sauce, cornstarch, sesame oil, 1/4 tsp baking soda & pepper, 2 tbsp oil, 2 garlic cloves, 1 tbsp ginger, 1 orange bell pepper (sliced), 1/2 onion (sliced), green onions (sliced), 1/2 cup orange juice, 1/4 cup soy sauce, 2 tbsp vinegar, 2 tbsp honey, 1 tbsp cornstarch, 1/4 cup water, 1/2 tsp flakes (opt), zest.

Instructions: 1. Marinate beef for at least 15 min. 2. Whisk together orange juice, soy sauce, rice vinegar, honey, cornstarch, water, and red pepper flakes (opt). 3. Fry the beef in 1 tbsp oil for 3-4 min per side or until browned. 4. Remove. 5. Fry garlic, ginger, pepper, onion for 2-3 min or until softened. 6. Pour the prepared sauce into the wok. 7. Bring to a simmer and cook for 1-2 min or until the sauce has thickened. 8. Return cooked beef to the wok and toss to coat in the sauce. 9. Cook for 1-2 min more, or until heated through. 10. Garnish with chopped green onions and orange zest. 11. Serve.

Nutritional info: 450 cal, 30g protein, 30g carbs, 22g fat, 2g fiber.

Honey Walnut Shrimp
Yields: 4 servings **Prep time:** 15 minutes **Total time:** 30 minutes **Equipment:** Wok, spatula, parchment paper.

Ingredients: 1 lb shrimp, 1/4 cup cornstarch, salt, pepper, 1/2 cup walnuts, 2 tbsp honey, 1 tbsp water, 2 tbsp oil, 2 minced garlic, 1 tbsp ginger, 1/4 cup honey, 2 tbsp mayo, 1 tbsp vinegar, 1 tbsp soy sauce, 1/4 tsp sesame oil, salt, green onions (chopped), sesame seeds (opt).

Instructions: 1. Coat shrimp. 2. Combine honey & water, add walnuts, coat, bake at 350°F until golden. 3. Fry shrimp in 1 tbsp oil. 4. In the same wok, add minced garlic and ginger. 5. Stir-fry for 30 sec or until fragrant. 6. Add 1/4 cup honey, mayonnaise, soy sauce, sesame oil, salt, and pepper. 7. Stir-fry for 1-2 min or until the sauce is heated through and combined. 8. Return shrimp and walnuts. 9. Toss. 10. Garnish and serve.

Nutritional info: 450 cal, 25g protein, 30g carbs, 25g fat, 2g fiber.

Lobster Cantonese

Yields: 2 servings **Prep time:** 15 minutes **Total time:** 30 minutes **Equipment:** Wok, spatula, knife/shears.

Ingredients: 2 lobsters, 3 tbsp oil, 4 minced garlic cloves, 1-inch ginger (sliced), 3 green onions (separated), bell peppers (sliced), 1/4 cup broth, 2 tbsp soy sauce, 1 tbsp oyster sauce, 1 tbsp rice wine, 1 tsp sugar, 1/4 tsp pepper, 1 tbsp cornstarch, 2 tbsp water.

Instructions: 1. Prep lobsters. 2. Whisk together soy sauce, oyster sauce, rice wine, sugar, black pepper, cornstarch, and water. 3. Fry lobster in 2 tbsp hot oil until cooked. 4. Remove. 5. Fry garlic, ginger, and white onions for 30 sec or until fragrant. 6. Add peppers and stir-fry for 2-3 min or until softened. 7. Pour the prepared sauce into the wok. 8. Bring to a simmer and cook for 1-2 min or until the sauce has thickened. 9. Return lobster. 10. Cook for 1-2 min more, or just until heated through. 11. Garnish and serve.

Nutritional info: 450 cal, 40g protein, 20g carbs, 25g fat, 1g fiber.

Mongolian Hot Pot

Yields: 4 servings **Prep time:** 20 minutes **Total time:** 40 minutes **Equipment:** Wok, spatula.

Ingredients: 1 lb lamb/beef, 1 tbsp soy sauce, cornstarch, 1/4 tsp pepper, 6 cups broth, 1 tbsp soy sauce, 1/4 cup rice wine, 1/2 tsp ginger, 2 garlic cloves, 2 tbsp oil, 1 onion, 8 oz mushrooms, 1 cup bok choy, 1/2 cup carrots, 8 oz cellophane noodles (opt), dipping sauces (opt).

Instructions: 1. Marinate meat for at least 15 min. 2. Simmer broth with soy sauce, wine, ginger, garlic. 3. Stir-fry meat in hot oil. 4. Remove. 5. Stir-fry onion, mushrooms, and carrots, then bok choy for 3-4 min or until veggies are tender-crisp. 6. Add veggies & meat to broth. 7. Add noodles (opt) and cook for 2-3 min or until softened. 8. Serve with dipping sauces (opt).

Nutritional info: 450-500 cal, 30-35g protein, 20-30g carbs, 20-25g fat, 2-3g fiber.

Korean BBQ

Yields: 4 servings **Prep time:** 20 minutes **Total time:** 35 minutes (including marinating)

Equipment: Wok, spatula.

Ingredients: 1 lb beef (ribeye/sirloin/short rib), marinade (1/4 cup soy sauce, 2 tbsp mirin, 2 tbsp brown sugar, 1 tbsp sesame oil, garlic, ginger, green onions, pepper), 1 tbsp oil, 1 onion, 2 cups mixed veggies, 1/4 cup water/broth, sesame seeds, green onions, kimchi (all optional garnish).

Instructions: 1. Marinate beef for at least 15 min. 2. Heat oil in a wok over medium-high heat. 3. Add marinated beef and cook in batches, stirring frequently, until browned. 4. Remove. 5. Fry onion and veggies for 2-3 min or until softened. 6. Return beef, add any remaining marinade & water/broth. 7. Cook for 1-2 min or until the sauce has thickened and the beef is heated through. 8. Garnish with sesame seeds, chopped green onions, and kimchi (opt). 9. Serve with rice.

Nutritional info: 450 cal, 30g protein, 25g carbs, 25g fat, 3g fiber.

Conclusion

Congratulations! You've taken the first step towards unlocking the extraordinary potential of your wok. As you've discovered, this versatile kitchen tool is more than just a pan; it's a gateway to a world of flavors, textures, and culinary creativity.

From the rapid-fire excitement of stir-frying to the gentle coaxing of delicate steaming, your wok can handle it all. Remember, the key to mastering this art lies in understanding the nuances of high-heat cooking. Experiment with different ingredients, explore diverse cuisines and don't be afraid to put your own spin on classic recipes.

Your wok is an invitation to culinary exploration. Let it inspire you to try new flavor combinations, experiment with different cooking techniques, and discover your unique culinary voice. As you gain confidence, you'll find yourself venturing beyond the familiar, creating dishes that surprise and delight your taste buds. Beyond the recipes in this book, we encourage you to embrace the joy of improvisation. Let the freshness of your ingredients guide your cooking. A handful of unexpected herbs or a splash of your favorite condiment can transform a simple dish into a culinary masterpiece.

Remember, every great chef started somewhere. With practice, patience, and a dash of enthusiasm, you'll be well on your way to becoming a wok master. The more you cook with your wok, the more intuitive it will become. You'll develop a feel for the heat, a sense of timing, and a deep understanding of how flavors meld together. Don't be afraid to make mistakes. Every kitchen mishap is an opportunity to learn and grow. The most important thing is to have fun and enjoy the process. Cooking should be a joyful experience, and your wok is the perfect tool for unleashing your inner culinary artist.

Thank you for buying this book! Please leave your honest review here to make our work better:

Stay tuned for our new books! Happy Cooking!

Appendixes

Glossary of Wok Cooking Terms

- **Braising (焖):** A slow-cooking method that involves first searing the food in a wok, then adding liquid and simmering until tender.

- **Deep-Fry (炸):** Submerging food in hot oil until cooked and crispy.

- **Deglaze:** The process of adding liquid (like wine, broth, or water) to a hot pan to loosen and dissolve browned bits of food stuck to the bottom, creating a flavorful sauce base.

- **Flash-Fry (爆):** A quick stir-frying technique where ingredients are cooked for a very short time over extremely high heat to preserve their texture and color.

- **Mise en Place:** A French term meaning "everything in its place." In cooking, it refers to the practice of preparing and organizing all ingredients before starting to cook.

- **Pan-Fry (煎):** Cooking food in a small amount of oil over medium heat, turning occasionally for even browning.

- **Seasoning (of the wok):** The process of coating a carbon steel wok with oil and heating it repeatedly to create a non-stick surface and prevent rust.

- **Steaming (蒸):** Cooking food in a steamer basket placed over simmering water in the wok. This is a gentle cooking method that preserves nutrients and flavors.

- **Stir-Fry (炒):** A high-heat cooking technique that involves rapidly tossing and stirring ingredients in a wok with a small amount of oil.

- **Velvet (Velveting) (滑炒):** A Chinese technique where meat or tofu is coated in cornstarch and briefly cooked in hot oil before stir-frying. This results in a tender, velvety texture.

- **Wok (鑊/鍋):** A round-bottomed cooking vessel with sloping sides, commonly used in Asian cuisines. It's ideal for stir-frying due to its large surface area and ability to conduct heat quickly.

- **Wok Hei (鍋氣/镬气):** Literally translates to "breath of the wok." This term refers to the smoky, charred aroma and flavor imparted to food when cooked over high heat in a wok. It's a hallmark of authentic stir-fries.

- **Wok Spatula (锅铲/鑊鏟):** A flat-bottomed spatula with a long handle designed for tossing and stirring ingredients in a wok.

Ingredient Substitutions

Vegetables:

- **Bok Choy:** Napa cabbage, Chinese broccoli (gai lan), or regular broccoli
- **Broccoli:** Cauliflower, broccolini, or asparagus
- **Carrots:** Zucchini, sweet potato, or winter squash
- **Mushrooms:** Any variety of edible mushrooms, like cremini, shiitake, or oyster mushrooms
- **Snow Peas:** Snap peas, green beans, or sugar snap peas
- **Bell Peppers:** Any color bell pepper or a combination
- **Water Chestnuts:** Bamboo shoots or jicama

Protein:

- **Chicken:** Pork, beef, shrimp, tofu, or tempeh
- **Beef:** Lamb, pork, or firm tofu
- **Pork:** Chicken, beef, or tempeh
- **Shrimp:** Scallops, white fish, or tofu

Aromatics:

- **Garlic:** Garlic powder (1/4 tsp per clove) or shallot
- **Ginger:** Ground ginger (1/4 tsp per tablespoon) or galangal
- **Green Onions:** Chives, leeks, or shallots
- **Chilies:** Red pepper flakes, chili powder, or hot sauce (adjust to taste)

Sauces & Condiments:

- **Soy Sauce:** Tamari (gluten-free), coconut aminos
- **Oyster Sauce:** Hoisin sauce, mushroom sauce (vegetarian)
- **Rice Vinegar:** White vinegar, apple cider vinegar, or white wine vinegar
- **Shaoxing Rice Wine:** Dry sherry, mirin, or sake
- **Chili Garlic Sauce:** Sriracha, sambal oelek, or other hot sauce

Other:

- **Cornstarch:** All-purpose flour, arrowroot powder, or potato starch (use slightly more)
- **Honey:** Maple syrup, agave nectar, or brown sugar
- **Peanut Butter:** Any nut butter or sunflower seed butter (for nut allergies)

Tips for Substitution:

- **Flavor:** Choose substitutes with similar flavor profiles.
- **Texture:** Consider the texture of the original ingredient and choose a substitute that will provide a similar mouthfeel.
- **Dietary Needs:** If you have dietary restrictions or allergies, select substitutes that meet your needs.
- **Taste Test:** Always taste your dish as you cook and adjust seasonings as needed.

Measurement Conversions

Volume:

- 1 tablespoon = 3 teaspoons
- 1/4 cup = 4 tablespoons
- 1/3 cup = 5 tablespoons + 1 teaspoon
- 1/2 cup = 8 tablespoons
- 2/3 cup = 10 tablespoons + 2 teaspoons
- 3/4 cup = 12 tablespoons
- 1 cup = 16 tablespoons

Weight:

- 1 ounce = 28 grams
- 1 pound = 16 ounces = 454 grams

Temperature:

- Water boils at 212°F (100°C)
- Oil for deep frying should be between 350°F (175°C) and 375°F (190°C)

Additional Tips:

- Invest in a kitchen scale for the most accurate measurements, especially when it comes to meat and fish.
- If you don't have measuring spoons or cups, use a regular spoon as a guide.
- Remember, cooking is all about experimentation and finding what works best for you. Feel free to adjust the measurements in recipes based on your own taste preferences.

Abbreviations

Abbreviation	Transcription
cal	calories
carbs	carbohydrates
g	grams
lb	pound
min	minute(s)
opt	optional
oz	ounce
qt	quart
sec	second(s)
tbsp	tablespoon
tsp	teaspoon

Recipe Index

Beef Dumplings (Jiaozi), 57
Chicken & Corn Soup (Wok-Style), 59
Coconut Curry Shrimp, 22
Coconut Curry Tempeh, 35
Dakgalbi (Spicy Stir-fried Chicken), 85
Garlic Ginger Broccoli, 29
Garlic Ginger Chicken, 38
Pineapple & Veggie Stir-fry, 32
Pineapple Fried Rice, 53
Green Curry, 81
Honey Soy Salmon, 21
Kung Pao Brussels Sprouts, 30
Maple Ginger Tempeh, 23
Panang Curry, 81
Ramen, 89
Quick Cashew Tofu, 18
Sesame Ginger Tofu, 32
Shrimp and Broccoli Stir-fry, 74
Speedy Shrimp Lo Mein, 17
Spicy Korean Beef, 41
Spicy Peanut Tofu, 33
Spicy Tofu Lettuce Wraps, 76
Szechuan Beef, 41
Sweet & Sour Cauliflower, 30
Teriyaki Tofu Blitz, 26
Tofu and Vegetable Soup, 74
Udon Stir-fry, 89
Vegetable Fried Rice, 53
Vegetable Lo Mein in a Flash, 26
Weeknight Chicken & Broccoli Stir-fry, 17
15-Minute Beef & Broccoli, 25

C
Cabbage
Chinese Cabbage Soup (Wok-Style), 60
Papaya Salad (Som Tum), 84
Mandu (Korean Dumplings), 87
Moo Shu Pork, 43
Pan-Fried Pork Dumplings (Pot Stickers), 55
Pork & Cabbage Dumplings (Jiaozi), 56
Spicy Korean Beef, 41
Spring Rolls, 79
Vegetable Dumplings (Jiaozi), 56
Yakisoba, 87
Carrots
Broccoli & Cashew Stir-fry, 30
Beef & Vegetable Soup (Wok-Style), 59
Chicken & Corn Soup (Wok-Style), 59
Chicken Fried Rice, 52
Dakgalbi (Spicy Stir-fried Chicken), 85
Egg Fried Rice, 53
Fast & Flavorful Vegetable Fried Rice, 18
Garlic Ginger Bok Choy, 21
Ginger Pork with Bok Choy, 45
Gyoza, 88
Honey Glazed Carrots & Snow Peas, 31

Broccoli & Cashew Stir-fry, 30
Hot & Sour Soup (Suan La Tang), 59
Papaya Salad (Som Tum), 84
Kimchi Fried Rice (Kimchi Bokkeumbap), 85
Mongolian Hot Pot, 95
Orange Beef Tenderloin, 94
Pancit Bihon, 51
Chicken Lettuce Wraps, 74
Chicken+Mushroom Stir-fry (light on the sauce), 77
Kung Pao Chicken (Wok-Style), 77
Quick Cashew Tofu, 18
Ramen, 89
Shrimp and Broccoli Stir-fry, 74
Shrimp Fried Rice, 52
Shrimp Lo Mein, 50
Spicy Korean Beef, 41
Spicy Peanut Noodles, 21
Spring Rolls, 79
Stir-fried Cabbage with Garlic, 75
Sweet & Sour Cauliflower, 30
Teriyaki Tofu Blitz, 26
Tofu and Vegetable Soup, 74
Udon Stir-fry, 89
Vegetable Fried Rice, 53
Vegetable Lo Mein in a Flash, 26
15-Minute Beef & Broccoli, 25
Cashews
Broccoli & Cashew Stir-fry, 30
Pineapple Fried Rice, 53
Quick Cashew Tofu, 18
Spicy Tofu Lettuce Wraps, 76
Tempeh Stir-fry with Cashews, 35
Cayenne pepper
Caramelized Bananas, 92
Chicken Satay, 83
Celery
Chow Mein, 78
Chicken
Weeknight Chicken & Broccoli Stir-fry, 17
Kung Pao Chicken in a Flash, 19
One-Pan Ginger Chicken with Bok Choy, 20
Orange Glazed Chicken, 23
Speedy Sesame Chicken, 25
Thai Basil Chicken Express, 27
Chicken Stir-Fries, 36
Cashew Chicken, 36
Orange Chicken, 36
Honey Garlic Chicken, 36
Lemon Chicken, 37
Sweet & Sour Chicken, 37
Thai Basil Chicken (Pad Krapow Gai), 37
Pineapple Chicken, 38
Black Pepper Chicken, 38
Garlic Ginger Chicken, 38
Chicken Lo Mein, 50

Cornflakes
Tteokbokki (Spicy Rice Cakes), 85
Kimchi Fried Rice (Kimchi Bokkeumbap), 85
Green beans
Broccoli & Cashew Stir-fry, 30
Chicken & Mushroom Stew (Wok-Style), 61
Coconut Curry Tempeh, 35
Green Bean & Pork Stir-fry, 45
Panang Curry, 81
Rainbow Veggie Medley, 29
Spicy Szechuan Green Beans, 29
Spicy Tempeh & Green Beans, 35
Thai Basil Chicken (Pad Krapow Gai), 37
Vegetable Spring Rolls, 73

H
Honey
Black Pepper Beef, 40
Braised Short Ribs, 64
Chicken & Corn Soup (Wok-Style), 59
Chicken Lettuce Wraps, 74
Chicken Satay, 83
Cold Sesame Noodles (with Wok-Toasted Sesame Oil), 76
Dakgalbi (Spicy Stir-fried Chicken), 85

Egg Fried Rice, 53
Garlic Ginger Chicken, 38
Garlic Honey Pork, 44
General Tso's Chicken, 78
General Tso's Sauce, 67
Ginger Beef, 40
Ginger Pork with Bok Choy, 45
Honey Garlic Pork Stir-fry, 27
Honey Glazed Apples, 92
Honey Glazed Carrots & Snow Peas, 31

Honey Mustard Dipping Sauce, 71
Honey Soy Salmon, 21
Honey Walnut Shrimp, 94
Lemon Chicken, 37
Mongolian Beef, 39
One-Pan Ginger Chicken with Bok Choy, 20
Orange Beef Tenderloin, 94
Orange Chicken, 36
Orange Glazed Chicken, 23
Orange Glazed Tempeh, 34
Pad See Ew, 82
Panang Curry, 81
Peanut Dipping Sauce, 69
Peanut Sauce, 68
Pineapple & Veggie Stir-fry, 32
Pineapple Chicken, 38
Pineapple Pork, 44
Pineapple Shrimp, 48
Quick Cashew Tofu, 18
Quick Spicy Peanut Noodles, 26

Sesame Dipping Sauce, 70
Sesame Ginger Soba Noodles, 89
Sesame Ginger Tofu, 32
Simple Sesame Noodles, 19
Speedy Sesame Chicken, 25
Spicy Beef Noodle Soup, 61
Spicy Chili Garlic Shrimp, 48
Spicy Garlic Sauce, 68
Spicy Peanut Noodles, 21
Spicy Peanut Tofu, 33
Spicy Tempeh & Green Beans, 35
Steamed Dumplings (Jiaozi), 75
Stir-fried Cabbage with Garlic, 75

Sweet & Sour Chicken, 37
Sweet & Sour Dipping Sauce, 71
Sweet & Sour Pork, 42
Sweet & Sour Shrimp, 46
Sweet Chili Dipping Sauce, 69
Teriyaki Chicken, 88
Teriyaki Sauce, 67

Teriyaki Tempeh, 34
Tofu & Vegetable Stir-fry, 73
K
Kimchi
Doenjang Jjigae (Soybean Paste Stew), 86
Kimchi Fried Rice (Kimchi Bokkeumbap), 85
Kimchi Jjigae (Kimchi Stew), 86
Korean BBQ, 95
Mandu (Korean Dumplings), 87
Kimchi juice
Kimchi Fried Rice (Kimchi Bokkeumbap), 85
Kimchi Jjigae (Kimchi Stew), 86
L
Lime
Mango Salsa Dipping Sauce, 71
Nasi Goreng, 54
Spicy Peanut Noodles, 21
Tom Yum Soup, 82
Lime juice
Green Curry, 81
Mango Salsa Dipping Sauce, 71
Panang Curry, 81
Peanut Dipping Sauce, 69
Pineapple Chicken, 38
Pineapple Pork, 44
Shrimp with Lobster Sauce, 47
Tom Yum Soup, 82
Lime leaves, kaffir
Panang Curry, 81
Tom Yum Soup, 82
Lobster
Ginger Scallion Lobster Rice, 54

Sesame Beef Strips, 22
Lobster Cantonese, 95
Lo mein noodles
Beef Lo Mein, 50
Chicken Lo Mein, 50
Shrimp Lo Mein, 50
Speedy Shrimp Lo Mein, 17
Vegetable Lo Mein, 72

M
Maple syrup
Caramelized Bananas, 92
Ginger Beef, 40
Honey Glazed Apples, 92
Maple Ginger Tempeh, 23
One-Pan Ginger Chicken with Bok Choy, 20
Orange Glazed Tempeh, 34
Quick Cashew Tofu, 18
Sesame Ginger Soba Noodles, 89
Simple Sesame Noodles, 19
Spicy Peanut Noodles, 21
Spicy Tempeh & Green Beans, 35
Sweet Chili Dipping Sauce, 69

Teriyaki Chicken, 88
Teriyaki Tempeh, 34
Marshmallow fluff/minis
Chocolate Wontons, 93
Mirin (sweet rice wine)
Bulgogi, 84
Easy Teriyaki Salmon, 19
Mongolian Beef, 39
Sesame Ginger Soba Noodles, 89
Teriyaki Chicken, 88
Teriyaki Tempeh, 34
Molasses
Gingerbread Stir-fry, 92
Mushrooms
15-Minute Beef & Broccoli, 25
Beef & Vegetable Soup (Wok-Style), 59
Beef Lo Mein, 50
Braised Tofu with Mushrooms, 63
Chicken & Corn Soup (Wok-Style), 59

Chicken & Mushroom Dumplings (Jiaozi), 57
Chicken & Mushroom Stir-fry (light on the sauce), 76
Chinese Cabbage Soup (Wok-Style), 60
Clear Broth Noodle Soup, 75
Doenjang Jjigae (Soybean Paste Stew), 86
Drunken Noodles (Pad Kee Mao), 51
Garlic Ginger Bok Choy, 21
Hot and Sour Soup, 79
Hot & Sour Soup (Suan La Tang), 59
Papaya Salad (Som Tum), 84
Kimchi Jjigae (Kimchi Stew), 86
Lemon Pepper Tofu Scramble, 28

Mongolian Hot Pot, 95
Mushroom & Asparagus Delight, 31
Nasi Goreng, 54
Pancit Bihon, 51
Ramen, 89
Seafood Tofu Soup, 60
Sesame Ginger Soba Noodles, 89

Speedy Shrimp Lo Mein, 17
Spicy Korean Beef, 41
Spring Rolls, 79
Teriyaki Tofu Blitz, 26
Tofu and Vegetable Soup, 74
Udon Stir-fry, 89
Vegetable Dumplings (Jiaozi), 56
Vegetable Fried Rice, 53
Vegetable Lo Mein in a Flash, 26
Weeknight Chicken & Broccoli Stir-fry, 17
Yangzhou Fried Rice, 54
Mussels
Doenjang Jjigae (Soybean Paste Stew), 86
Haemul Pajeon (Seafood Pancake), 87

N
Napa cabbage
Chinese Cabbage Soup (Wok-Style), 60
Gyoza, 88
Mandu (Korean Dumplings), 87
Moo Shu Pork, 43
Pan-Fried Pork Dumplings (Pot Stickers), 55
Pork & Cabbage Dumplings (Jiaozi), 56
Noodles (ramen, udon, etc.)
15-Minute Beef & Broccoli, 25
Beef & Vegetable Soup (Wok-Style), 59
Beef Dumplings (Jiaozi), 57
Beef Lo Mein, 50
Beef with Snow Peas, 42
Black Pepper Beef, 40
Black Pepper Shrimp, 47
Chicken & Mushroom Stew (Wok-Style), 61
Chicken Lo Mein, 50
Chow Mein, 78
Cold Sesame Noodles (with Wok-Toasted Sesame Oil), 76
Drunken Noodles (Pad Kee Mao), 51
Egg Fried Rice, 53
Garlic Honey Pork, 44
Ginger Pork with Bok Choy, 45
Honey Garlic Chicken, 36
Kung Pao Chicken (Wok-Style), 77
Kung Pao Pork, 43
Lamb Dumplings (Jiaozi), 58
Lemon Chicken, 37
Mongolian Beef, 39
Nasi Goreng, 54

Mango Salsa Dipping Sauce, 71
Orange Beef Tenderloin, 94
Pad See Ew, 82
Pan-Fried Pork Dumplings (Pot Stickers), 55
Pancit Bihon, 51
Pepper Steak, 39
Quick Spicy Peanut Noodles, 26
Ramen, 89

Seafood Tofu Soup, 60
Sesame Beef Strips, 22
Sesame Ginger Soba Noodles, 89
Simple Sesame Noodles, 19
Shrimp & Chive Dumplings (Har Gow), 55
Shrimp & Snow Peas, 49
Shrimp Fried Rice, 52
Shrimp Lo Mein, 50
Shrimp with Lobster Sauce, 47
Spicy Beef Noodle Soup, 61
Spicy Chili Garlic Noodles, 24
Spicy Chili Garlic Shrimp, 48
Spicy Korean Beef, 41
Spicy Peanut Noodles, 21
Spicy Tempeh & Green Beans, 35
Steamed Dumplings (Jiaozi), 75
Teriyaki Chicken, 88
Teriyaki Tofu Blitz, 26
Tofu and Vegetable Soup, 74
Twice-Cooked Pork (Hui Guo Rou), 43
Udon Stir-fry, 89
Vegetable Dumplings (Jiaozi), 56
Vegetable Fried Rice, 53
Vegetable Lo Mein in a Flash, 26
Vegetable Spring Rolls, 73
Wok-Fired Drunken Noodles (Pad Kee Mao), 80
Yangzhou Fried Rice, 54

Nori
Ramen, 89
Nutmeg
Apple Cinnamon Spring Rolls, 93
Caramelized Bananas, 92
Gingerbread Stir-fry, 92
Nuts
Chocolate Wontons, 93
Gingerbread Stir-fry, 92
Mango Salsa Dipping Sauce, 71
Nasi Goreng, 54
Peanut Dipping Sauce, 69
Pineapple Fried Rice, 53
Spicy Peanut Noodles, 21
Spicy Tofu Lettuce Wraps, 76
Sweet Sesame Balls (Jin Deui), 91

O
Orange juice
Orange Beef Tenderloin, 94

Orange Glazed Tempeh, 34
Orange Sauce, 67
Orange zest
Lemon Garlic Shrimp, 47
Orange Beef Tenderloin, 94
Orange Chicken, 36
Orange Glazed Tempeh, 34

P
Panko breadcrumbs
Chicken Katsu, 88
Gingerbread Stir-fry, 92
Papaya, green
Papaya Salad (Som Tum), 83
Peanut butter
Peanut Dipping Sauce, 69
Spicy Peanut Noodles, 21
Spicy Tofu Lettuce Wraps, 76
Peanuts, roasted
Haemul Pajeon (Seafood Pancake), 87
Kung Pao Brussels Sprouts, 30
Kung Pao Chicken (Wok-Style), 77
Nasi Goreng, 54
Pineapple Fried Rice, 53
Spicy Peanut Noodles, 21
Spicy Tofu Lettuce Wraps, 76
Peas
Broccoli & Cashew Stir-fry, 30
Chicken & Corn Soup (Wok-Style), 59
Chicken Fried Rice, 52
Coconut Curry Tempeh, 35
Dakgalbi (Spicy Stir-fried Chicken), 85
Egg Fried Rice, 53
Garlic Ginger Bok Choy, 21
Ginger Pork with Bok Choy, 45
Honey Glazed Carrots & Snow Peas, 31
Mongolian Hot Pot, 95
Nasi Goreng, 54
Panang Curry, 81
Pineapple & Veggie Stir-fry, 32
Pineapple Fried Rice, 53
Rainbow Veggie Medley, 29
Ramen, 89
Shrimp & Snow Peas, 49
Shrimp Fried Rice, 52
Shrimp Lo Mein, 50
Spicy Korean Beef, 41
Spicy Peanut Noodles, 21
Super Simple Shrimp & Snow Peas, 28
Udon Stir-fry, 89
Vegetable Fried Rice, 53

Vegetable Lo Mein in a Flash, 26
Yangzhou Fried Rice, 54
Peppercorns, Sichuan

Made in the USA
Las Vegas, NV
27 November 2024

12834130R00063